STUART MCHARDY is a writer, occasional bⁱ

been actively involved in many aspects of Scottish culture throughout his adult life – music, poetry, language, history, folklore – he has been resident in Edinburgh for over a quarter of a century. Although he has held some illustrious positions including Director of the Scots Language Resource Centre in Perth and President of the Pictish Arts Society, McHardy is probably proudest of having been a member of the Vigil for a Scottish Parliament. Often to be found in the bookshops, libraries and tea-rooms of Edinburgh, he lives near the city centre with the lovely (and ever-tolerant) Sandra and they have one son, Roderick.

The Pagan Symbols
of the Picts

STUART McHARDY

Luath Press Limited

EDINBURGH

www.luath.co.uk

First published 2012
New edition 2015
Reprinted 2016

ISBN: 978-1-910021-75-0

The paper used in this book is sourced from renewable forestry

and is FSC credited material

Printed and bound by
Bell & Bain Ltd., Glasgow

Typeset in 11 point Sabon
by 3btype.com

Contents

Preface

GIVEN THE LENGTH of time since they were created and the lack of direct written evidence concerning the Pictish symbols, some of their meanings are more opaque than others. My interpretations in some cases have extensive support within early texts while in other instances much of what I suggest is almost completely speculative and perhaps incapable of any real extent of proof. Hopefully, with the increasing sophistication of archaeological methodologies and the development of new techniques, our understanding will be improved. However, I hope the approach adopted here can lead to a clearer vision of what the symbols may mean, and thus may help us gain a clearer understanding of the inhabitants of 1st millennium Scotland and earlier.

The ideas presented in this book have developed over nearly 40 years of study and contemplation and thus any mistakes are mine alone. Where I have quoted others, this is in support of my contentions and it should not be assumed that those quoted agree with all, or even any, of what is presented herein. Having taken a university degree in history, I am aware that most of what is called history has been written at the behest of what can only be called 'elites'. Because of this, much of what passes for human history, and indeed archaeology, is overly concerned with earlier elites, even where there is no hard evidence that they existed. Most history books until relatively recently paid little attention to anyone other than elite groups of males between their late teens and middle age. Women generally are only noticed in detail when they are fulfilling a role normally assumed to be a masculine one and there are few, if any, mentions of other women, children, healers, poets, musicians, farmers, fisherfolk, craftspeople and many other groups in society.

Historians have long been obsessed with what they perceive as elite behaviour, though the growth of social history over the past half century is beginning to give us a more rounded picture of what the past was like.

In this work I draw heavily upon material that initially survived through oral transmission and was thus not subject to the control of religious, military or economic elites, as written history has always been. In *A New History of the Picts,* I have gone so far as to suggest that in tribal Britain the modern concept of the elite would have been anachronistic and is unhelpful in trying to understand our common past. At least some of my ancestors were Picts – the name McHardy seems to have originated in what was the Pictish province of Mar – but some were Irish and, according to family tradition, there are Norse antecedents in there too. However, I make no claim to being a Pict, or even a Celt, a term that has no ethnic significance whatsoever. I am a Scot who believes that the past of my country has been badly interpreted and considerably misunderstood and it is in pursuit of a greater understanding of that past that I have developed the ideas here presented.

Thanks, as ever, are due to the Luath crew for teasing this work into print. Additionally thanks to Nick Simpson and Davie Moir for help with illustrations and stimulating discussions. Thanks to my long-term Pictish colleague Nick Simpson for his help with the images throughout the book and a thank you to Dave Moir for helping me clarify my thoughts.

Stuart McHardy

Introduction

Methodology

DUE TO THE lack of early written Scottish sources it has been
necessary for commentators on our past to look elsewhere for
historical sources. In the main, this has in effect been the Roman
Empire, England and Ireland, simply because there are surviving
early sources from all three. It is ironic that so many have used
English sources considering the role played by Edward I and later
Cromwellian troops in destroying what did exist of early documen-
tation in Scotland. Although the material emanating from the early
Irish annals is of considerable importance, it is my contention that
far too much attention has been paid to the supposed influence of
Ireland on Scotland. In his article 'Were The Scots Irish?' (2000)
Ewan Campbell of Glasgow University has, I believe, totally
debunked the notion that Dalriada, the Scottish society based
around the Kilmartin valley in the 1st Millennium, was founded by
invaders from Ulster *c.*500CE. He points out that there is no
contemporary historical, archaeological or linguistic evidence that
supports the contention that the Scots arrived from Ireland, and
goes so far as to suggest that there was in fact considerable cultural
and political influence in the opposite direction. Further, I would
suggest that the many references in histories of the period to the
Kingdoms of Dalriada and Pictland is, for reasons that will become
clear, unhelpful in understanding how those societies functioned,
and for much of the 1st Millennium is simply inaccurate.

The Romans describe tribal societies. As late as the 18th century
tribal society still flourished in much of the Scottish mainland. Are
we to believe it disappeared and then returned? This is unheard of
in the human story. Therefore we must surely accept that in some

ways the tribal societies of late Medieval Scotland developed over time from those earlier tribal societies described by the Romans. From what we can tell, those societies were non-literate when the Romans arrived and it was only with the introduction of Christianity that the written word appeared amongst the native peoples. And for long enough after that, reading and writing was the sole prerogative of churchmen; churchmen who, from the Synod of Whitby in 664, owed their allegiance to an organisation centred in far off Rome, and whose writings are unashamedly propagandistic. God was, after all, on their side.

It is one of the major mistakes of historians to assume that once literature is introduced into society, oral tradition either disappears or is discredited. For many millennia such societies as did exist in what we now call Scotland were held together by myths and legends, stories and tales, that could only pass from lip to ear. Evidence from Australia illustrates that oral transmission can carry accurate information over tens of thousands of years (Isaacs 1991), but here I would mention the case of Troy. Troy was found not by professional archaeologists or historians but by a German industrialist Heinrich Schliemann who, despite the objections of the professionals, had decided that the tales Homer spun into the Iliad were based on fact. To the academic establishment of his day, Homer's sources were 'just stories'. That is a fair description of much of the material that I have used to try to tease out meaning from the symbols of the Picts, and it is worth remembering that we too have at least one Pictish instance of the viability of traditional tales. Norrie's Law was long said to be the burial site of a warrior, traditionally a Danish rather than a Pictish warrior, who was buried in a suit of silver armour. The veracity of this can be checked by looking at the remnants of the silver found in the tumulus, now on show in the Museum of Scotland.

History is limited by the tyranny of the written word. As Campbell (supra) and others have shown, the written word is often little more than propaganda. We have to be critical in our approach to the written word and this applies just as much to words written down that were once spoken as story. Wherever possible I have considered a variety of sources, temporal and geographic, in suggesting possible direct links to what we can only call pagan belief. The general meaning of pagan here is pre-Christian, and where I go further to suggest specific possibilities and relationships, I should re-emphasise that this is derived from my own thinking. According to the *Compact Edition of the Oxford English Dictionary* (OED) the term pagan originally had the sense of

> ... villager, rustic... indicating the fact that the ancient idolatry lingered on in the rural villages and hamlets after Christianity had been generally accepted in the towns and cities of the Roman Empire
>
> 1979, p.2052

Given that Scotland had very few towns or cities until well into the medieval period this seems particularly apt. By analysing material that emanated from the traditional stories, myths and legends of Wales, Ireland and Scandinavia I hope I can show that we can put together a model for understanding something of what the symbols may have meant to the people who created them.

One of the reasons for investigating the pre-Christian Picts is to develop a picture that archaeologists can perhaps use to pose questions about sites from pagan times. In order to develop such a picture I have spent considerable effort trying to understand not only how relevant information can be transmitted through the oral tradition, but also in analysing the Scottish landscape in the light of putative pagan belief. Through a combination of approaches, I have come up with an interpretation of the Pictish past which, correct or not, has the advantage of being cohesive and as such might well fill the role of stimulating further discussion and hopefully begin to provide a framework that might allow the development of a specific Scottish archaeological approach to the Picts.

Map of sites mentioned in the text

1	Abernethy
2	Achnabreck
3	Ardross
4	Bennachie
5	Burghead
6	Collessie
7	Congash
8	Clynemilton
9	Drimmies
10	Dull
11	Dumbarton
12	Dunachton
13	Dunadd
14	Dunrobin
15	Easterton of Roseisle
16	Eday
17	Eildon Hills
18	Grantown
19	Glamis
20	Inverurie
21	Kintore
22	Kintradwell
23	Knocknagael
24	Latheron
25	Lindores
26	Logie Elphinstone
27	Meigle
28	Moy
29	Newton
30	North Berwick Law
31	Paps of Fife
32	Paps of Jura
33	Rhynie
34	St Vigean's
35	Sandside
36	Strathpeffer

CHAPTER ONE

Who were the Picts?

THE QUESTION OF who the Picts were has been the cause of much controversy over the years. The lack of early written material from Scotland has meant we have virtually no direct historical evidence regarding the Picts. This vacuum has served to create a situation where a whole range of theories have arisen regarding the origin of the Picts. Short of any evidence pointing to a major population influx in Scottish pre-history, and to date this has not been presented, it seems to me that the most sensible approach is to consider the Picts as the descendants of the original inhabitants of this part of the world (McHardy 2010).

Given that we now know that stories can pass down provable facts over millennia (Isaacs 1991), there may in fact be a hint as to their origin in the far past. The tradition given by Bede, a monk writing in Jarrow monastery in the 9th century, is that the Picts came from Scythia. In the 1st Millennium and into the Early Medieval period, Scythia referred, not to the area north of the Black Sea, but to the southern area of Scandinavia, modern Denmark and the adjoining areas. For a considerable period after the close of the last Ice Age, much of the area that is now the North Sea was dry land and it seems likely that people travelled east from Denmark and the Low Countries to Britain as well as coming into what is now England from the south.

The idea that people only came into Scotland after having come first into England has no specific evidence to support it. While some people probably did come by this route, early settlers were just as likely to have come in across the land bridge from the Continent. The geneticist Stephen Oppenheimer states that according to genetic analysis there was an influx of people from northern Norway as early as 4000BCE (2006, p.190) Given that Isaacs (1991, *passim*) has shown that stories containing factual, provable data have survived upwards of 30,000 years in Australia, the idea that memories of such an event could survive for 10,000 years in Scotland is hardly impossible.

The first written references we have to people in this part of the world come from the Romans. They called the people here Caledonians and Picts. In fact, the terms seem to have been inter-changeable and were applied effectively to the entire population north of Hadrian's Wall. In their references to the people here they seem to have been using both terms as generic descriptors of the tribal peoples they came across. While the Romans were only in Scotland for one extended period – nowadays the Antonine Wall is seen as having lasted no more than about 15 to 20 years at the most (McCann 1988), and the campaign of Severus lasted only a few seasons in the early 3rd century – they do tell us quite a lot about the inhabitants.

This is from the Roman Dio Cassius writing at the beginning of the 3rd century CE,

> There are two principal tribes of the Britons, the Caledonii and the Maeatae, and the names of the others have been merged in these two. The Maeatae live next to the cross-wall which cuts the island in half, and the Caledonians are beyond them. Both tribes inhabit wild and waterless mountains and desolate swampy plains, and possess neither walls, cities, nor tilled fields, but live on their flocks, wild game, and certain fruits; for they do not touch the fish which are found in immense and inexhaustible quantities. They dwell in tents, naked and unshod, possess their women in common and in common rear all their offspring. Their form of rule is democratic for the most part, and they are fond of plundering; consequently they choose their boldest men as rulers. They go into battle in chariots, and have small swift horses; there are also foot soldiers, very swift in running and very firm in standing their ground. For arms

they have a shield and a short spear, with a bronze apple attached to the end of the spear-shaft, so that when it is shaken it may clash and terrify the enemy; and they also have daggers. They can endure hunger and cold and any kind of hardship; for they plunge into the swamps and exist there for many days with only their heads above water, and in the forests they support themselves upon bark and roots, and for all emergencies they prepare a certain kind of food, the eating of a small portion of which, the size of a bean, prevents them from feeling either hunger or thirst.

1927, p.264

This is a description of a tribal warrior society and in the 2nd century, the Roman geographer Ptolemy gave a list of what were supposed to be the dominant tribes throughout the north of the British Isles. The interpretation of what were essentially tribal areas as being in some way akin to modern nation states with defined boundaries and centralised political structures is anachronistic, certainly before the 7th century when the expanding Northumbrians perhaps began to force the natives of Scotland into tighter political and military alignments. Dio Cassius also tells us that one of the two main tribes of the Caledonians, the Maetae, lived up against the wall, that cuts the island in half' (Ibid.). He was writing in 217CE, half a century after the Antonine Wall was finally abandoned, so is clearly writing about Hadrian's Wall. The Maetae are generally accepted as the equivalent of the southern Picts so what this tells us is that, certainly from the Roman point of view, the Picts were the inhabitants of all of what we now think of as Scotland. Folklore talks of Pechs or Pechts from the Borders to Shetland. From this perspective, the Scots can be understood as one of the Pictish tribes, and certainly as part of the Pictish world.

The reference by Cassius to the Caledonians being democratic is easily understood. We know that well into the late Medieval period the Highland tribes of Scotland, by now called clans, had an element of election in the selection of their chiefs and this is in fact common to tribal structures across the globe. Effectively, tribes are groups of inter-related families occupying specific territory and usually claiming descent from a common ancestor. The tribe or clan is defined by its strength in warriors, as well as its wealth in cattle, and the warriors are related by blood. The role of the chief in such societies is defined as much by duties as by rights. While he is the undoubted leader of his people he is also of them, as opposed to over them. Even into the 18th century there are instances of clan chiefs being dismissed from their positions, one particularly well-known instance (Scott 1843, p.47ff.) being simply because the chief appeared to his kin to have the wrong attitude towards his position! It would be wrong to think of Cassius's description of the Caledonian tribes being democratic as suggesting they were akin to modern Western societies or even Greek city states, but it does suggest that such governance as did exist amongst the natives of early Scotland may well have been akin to the *Things* we know existed amongst that other warrior people of Scotland, the Vikings. The *Things* were assemblies where situations were extensively debated by a considerable section of the community before decisions were taken as to what action was required. In Scotland the place-name Dingwall in Easter Ross, an area controlled by the Norsemen for centuries, refers directly to this practice.

The idea that tribes are primitive societies run by absolute despots has no support. Tribal societies are based on sophisticated social arrangements where all members of the group are bound together by often complex arrangements of mutual duties and rights. This was nowhere more so than in Scotland, where the tribal system survived into the second half of the 18th century, even if by then it was in terminal decline. There is no reason to think that the medieval clan societies of the Scottish Highlands were not the direct descendants of the earlier tribal structures amongst the Picts, and, in the west, the Scots.

In this respect it is worth remembering that the term *ri*, the Gaelic usage of which has always been translated as meaning king, has a different meaning in the P-Celtic languages and means lord,

or perhaps even chief. In many of the tales collected by John
Francis Campbell as *Popular Tales of the West Highlands* and *More
West Highland Tales* (Campbell 1994), actions attributed to kings,
queens, princes and princesses are often remarkably mundane and
might be better understood as referring to chiefs whose day-to-day
lives might not have differed much from those of their clansmen,
rather than those of beings whose very situation set them apart
from the rest of society.

When Cassius tells us that they choose their boldest men as
leaders he is underlining the point that at the reported battle of
Mons Graupius the Caledonians were led by Calgacus, who is not
referred to as king, emperor or even chief. He is clearly a war
leader and this is something that also survived into clan times.
Chiefs were expected in their youth to lead a raid to show their
skill and courage, but each clan had a specific captain who was in
charge of their fighting activities. This is only sensible. The entire
clan were bound by ties of blood and common ancestry, and it
would make sense for the community of warriors to be led by the
best man for the job. The idea that the hereditary chief was always
the leader in battle misinterprets the functioning of tribal society.

Cassius's point that they are 'fond of plundering' is also remarkably like the government descriptions of Highland clans in the
17th and 18th centuries as little more than 'cattle thieves'. I have
written of this elsewhere (McHardy 2004) but suffice it to say that
one of the most important regular activities of the warriors of the
clans was 'lifting' the cattle of other clans. This was not a criminal
act but an exercise in military skill and was a fundamental aspect
of the training of all warriors. Solinus *c.*250CE tells us that in the
Hebrides

Next come the iles called Hebudes [*Ebudes*] five in number,
the inhabitants whereof, know not what corne meaneth but
live onely by fishe and milke. They are all undere the government of one king, for as many of them as bee, they are
severed but with a narrow groope one from another. The

king hath nothing of hys own, but taketh from every mans. Hee is bound to equitie by certaine lawes: and lest he may start from right through covetousness, he learneth justice by povertie, as who may have nothing proper or peculiar to himselfe, but is found at the charges of the Realme.

Golding 1587, p.22

Although he uses the term for king, *rex*, this is clearly a tribal society where the leader is responsible to the population as a whole. This is something that is also echoed in later times when the clan system developed. Clan, *Clann*, in Gaelic, means 'the children' and makes it plain that the leader of that society is to a considerable extent the steward working on behalf of the children to come, just as he had to honour the ancestors that had gone before. The following is from Burt's *Letters to A Gentleman*, written in the 1720s

This power of the chiefs is not supported by Interest, as they are landlords, but as lineally descended from the old Patriarchs or Fathers of the Families; for they hold the same Authority when they have lost their Estates, as may appear from several, and particularly one who commands his Clan, though, at the same Time, they maintain him, having nothing left of his own.

On the other hand, the Chief, even against the Laws, is to protect his followers, as they are sometimes called, be they never so criminal.

1998, p.193

Here I believe that Burt misunderstands clan society. What is criminal to him was not criminal by the laws and customs of the clans. I suggest that while the clans were not precisely the same as the tribal arrangements of Pictish times, they had in fact developed from them and there is no evidence I can find to the contrary.

I have suggested this tribal society as a model for understanding 'Dark Age' Scotland (McHardy 2010) in terms of a series of inter-related and relatively stable kin groups. These societies were both P- and Q-Celtic-speaking with the Q-Celtic Scots being resident in the West. Differences in sound between the languages led to them being called P- and Q-Celtic because in Gaelic, Irish and Manx many words begin with the 'k' sound, while similar Welsh and Breton begin with a 'p'. The word Celtic was chosen in the 18th century to represent these in north-west European languages and the term has no actual ethnic value whatsoever. Recent research is underlining the idea that Germanic languages were known in Britain long before the arrival of the Romans (English URL; Fowler 1943). As this fits in with Oppenheimer's findings of genetic evidence for settlement in Scotland from northern Norway in the distant prehistoric past, it is likely that there were some Germanic speakers in the east of Scotland, and certainly in the northern isles of Orkney and Shetland. The barbarian conspiracy of 365CE was composed of Picts, Scots and Attacotti, according to the Romans they attacked. We have no other references to the Attacotti in Britain and it is worth considering whether they were in fact either a Germanic-speaking people or even Continental warriors, as there was a simultaneous attack on the Roman frontier in Germany. Apart from the early prehistoric arrivals from Norway we know that there were contacts between the coastal parts of the British Isles, Continental Europe, Scandinavia and even Africa from the Megalithic Age on, 3,000 years before the Pictish period.

One problem that faces us is that the Pictish Symbols are found almost exclusively north of the Forth-Clyde axis, and this distribution has understandably been the focus of much study. However, the only specific political demarcation from the Dark Age period in Scotland is the temporary Antonine Wall, just to the south of that part of Scotland where political and military struggle continued to erupt into battle till the 18th century. In the analysis presented here the ideas concerning possible remnants of a truly ancient religion apply as much to the tribes of southern Scotland, Damnonni, Novantae, Selgovae and Votadini that Ptolemy noted in the 2nd century, as to the tribal peoples to the north, and west. Likewise, the traditional dating of the Pictish period from 297 is arbitrary and unhelpful – the reference from then is to Caesar having fought the Picts – and a more suitable date for the commencement of the Pictish period, suggested by Smyth, would be the Battle of Mons Graupius, c.80BCE. However, there seems to be no good reason why we should put such a specific limit on the Pictish period as it seems clear to me that the Picts were the indigenous people of Scotland when the Romans arrived, and as such were the direct descendants of the first settlers after the Ice Age, no doubt intermingled with later small-scale groups of incomers. Or as the wisdom of the tradition has it, we are all Jock Tamson's bairns.

When the Romans first arrived in Britain it is obvious that the population was essentially tribal. The people were living in close-linked kin groups, in what was essentially a subsistence economy. This does not mean there were no luxuries. It simply means that the people lived in small groups and effectively fended for themselves, without centralised city-states and their political appurtenances. They were pastoralists, much of whose energy was focussed on the raising of cattle, but the role of hunting and foraging was an everyday part of their lives, and crops had been grown in Scotland since much earlier times. Recent archaeological thinking is that the old picture of the past in which such tribal peoples were constantly in fear of invasion and attack and whose lives were nasty, brutish and short contains very little substance. Much of such thinking seems to have arisen from the essentially Victorian idea of progress, wherein humanity was presented as growing steadily from a primitive and barbaric state towards ever more technologically advanced civilisation. Given today's problems with the consequent pollution and climate change, this idea of progress would appear to have lost some of its attraction.

However, even before the Egyptians started building pyramids the people of Britain had created such monumental and magnificent sites as Calanais in the Outer Hebrides, Macs Howe, Stennes and the increasingly important Brodgar sites in Orkney, the New Grange complex north of Dublin, and Stonehenge on the Salisbury plain. Whatever these remote ancestors of ours were, they were neither crude nor stupid. The sophistication of these structures has been interpreted as a clear indication that contemporary societies were under the control of religious or political elites. This is not the only interpretation. Cultural anthropology has shown us that in many tribal societies, communal working is an integral part of social existence, and though there may be a leader in performing any particular task, this does not make such a person a member of an elite class, merely the best person for the job. This communalism survives in Scotland amongst crofting communities where the idea of working together for mutual benefit has never been totally eroded. It was an integral part of clan society in the Highlands of Scotland that existed into the 18th century, which in many ways seems to have preserved structures of tribal behaviour that stemmed from long before the Romans arrived in these islands.

Another idea that is at last passing away is that the seas and rivers were barriers to prehistoric peoples. The absolute contrary now seems to be the real story – seas and rivers were in fact the highways of the ancient world (Cunliffe 2001, *passim*). This has considerable significance for how we interpret life in Scotland in the 1st Millennium BCE. Historically, Scotland has had strong links with both the Baltic nations and the Low Countries from Early Medieval times. It is in fact as easy and quick to sail to the Netherlands as to London at certain times of the year. However, we also know that trade, in such 'magical' substances as amber and gold, was taking place in the 2nd Millennium BCE and probably much earlier. Given what we now know about the abilities of ancient sailors, the necessity of hugging coastlines no longer seems as important as it was once thought. In terms of understanding Pictish society, this raises some intriguing possibilities.

Archaeology shows that there was contact between the people in Scotland and Continental Europe since the time when the great Megalithic structures of Calanais, Maes Howe and elsewhere were erected. The spread of Megalithic culture, including New Grange in Ireland and Stonehenge in England, ran from Scandinavia to

Morocco, underlining the reality that Scotland was never a completely isolated place, her location at the edge of the ocean making her accessible and not the opposite. And, as noted above, recent genetic research points to the fact that at least some of our ancestors arrived from northern Norway over 6,000 years ago. We should also remember that there have been suggestions that the Megalithic culture itself originated in Orkney.

Roman sources tell us that attacks were mounted from the North of Britain against them by barbarian tribes during the entire period of their occupation of southern Britain. Such attacks were frequent and at the very least show a capacity for working together amongst peoples, the Picts and Scots, whom we have been accustomed to understand as distinct ethnic groups and, essentially, enemies. We find them working together to attack Rome, there are clear instances of intermarriage, and it was these two tribal peoples who eventually merged to become the nation state of Scotland. In the 'barbarian conspiracy' we can perhaps see a convenient alliance between indigenous peoples and some of the Germanic-speaking troops brought into Britain from Europe by the Romans themselves. Another possibility, given the ages-old contacts over the North Sea, is that this alliance was founded on established links between the tribal peoples of Scotland and north-western Europe. Perhaps the situation was more like a combination of these two positions. The possibility that there were settlements of Germanic-speaking peoples on the east coast of Scotland during, or even considerably before, the Roman period, can no longer be ruled out. Such Celtic–Germanic linkage is distinctly possible given that we know that the great flowering of Gaelic culture under the Lordship of the Isles was based on a society that was truly Gall-Gael – a combination of Germanic- and Gaelic-speaking peoples. To this day many Scottish clans still claim descent from Norse ancestors.

Probably because the British Empire was essentially monoglot – people from Jamaica to Jawalpindi, from Ontario to Adelaide all learned to communicate through English – there has been general acceptance in the United Kingdom that in the past people lived in monoglot cultures. From this it is an easy step to defining peoples by the language they speak – so we have Gaels, Britons, Anglo-Saxons etc. However, in many parts of the world, multi-lingualism is the norm and we cannot state with any certainty that this was not the case in Dark Age Scotland. After all, we know that there was contact between Ireland and the Baltic, and the Megalith builders were part of a culture that stretched as far as North Africa. In this respect, an interesting Lewis tradition speaks of the Calanais stones having been raised initially by men who were black. Similarities in weaponry, hill fort building and pottery-making techniques between Britain and adjoining Europe have been noted by archaeologists, and if one leaves out the question of language, there were a great many similarities indeed between all of the tribal peoples living round the coasts of the North Sea.

Although nowadays we use words like Celtic and Anglo-Saxon as if they had an ethnic component, we should remember that these words are effectively descriptive only of language. The people of the Dark Age tribes and earlier would have had no over-arching sense of community beyond their own kin and would in all likelihood be as liable to form alliances with people who spoke a different language as with those who spoke a dialect of their own, depending on circumstances. In his work *The Atlantic Celts*, Professor Simon James makes the salient point that the term Celtic would have meant nothing to any Welsh or Gaelic speaker before the 18th century. The notion of the Celtic nations is entirely a 20th century construct. That there were close relationships between Scotland's west coast tribes and those in Ireland is however indisputable; people from both sides of the North Channel have probably been intermarrying for much of the last four or five millennia – and both communities were clearly part of the 3rd millennium BCE megalithic tradition. Communication between Scotland's west coast, the Isle of Man and Wales were a regular fact of life. The fact that Galloway, Kintyre and Ulster are all in sight of each other in fair weather, and that we know people were sailing these waters since at least the 4th Millennium BCE, underlines this.

In his 7th century *Life of Columba* Adomnan mentions, in passing, a trading ship from Gaul visiting Iona. On the east coast communication across the North Sea was taking place long before the Dark Ages and the development of inter-tribal links seems something that must have happened. In this respect some of the ideas of the origins of the Picts can be put in context.

In the past, historical changes have often been presented as resulting from incursions by technologically superior, aristocratic groups who effectively took over indigenous society. While this fantasy had undoubted appeal for the class-ridden elite of the British Empire, it is hardly a sustainable picture of what actually happened. Scottish history, with Scotland being an integral, indeed vital, part of a successful Empire, has tended to reflect the ideas of that Empire. Accordingly, we have had several centuries of interpretation of Highland society as being in some way feudal. This is utterly unsustainable and reflective more of the history of England than Scotland. British history has tended to be not much more than English history writ large. Tribal societies are based on kinship; feudalism is based on kingship. This is relevant because what we actually know of the Highland clan system as it survived into the 18th century, can perhaps give us some sense of how people were living in what we call the Dark Ages, when tribal existence was the norm in North Britain. For instance, we know that several distinct clans could unite when they felt it necessary. The Farquharsons, MacGillivrays, MacIntoshes, MacPhersons and Shaws were all part of the tribal confederation of *Clan Chattan* while the Grants, MacAlpines, MacAulays, MacGregors, MacKinnons, MacNabs, Macphies and Macquarries were all part of *Siol Alpine*, the seed or descendants of Alpin. It is also of interest that different clans claim their origins as Gall-Gael, Pictish and Norse. None of them claim any descent from Saxons but it is worth considering how much Roman historians, writing far from Scotland, and with no first-hand experience, could be aware of tribal or territorial distinctions among either the Germanic- or the Celtic-speaking peoples.

The reality of tribal society is that it is kin-based, egalitarian to some extent, and remarkably tenacious. All the members of the tribe (excepting those marrying in or entering the tribe from elsewhere), claimed descent from one common ancestor and they were thus, at least in theory, related to one another. The status of the later Highland chiefs, particularly when they were outwith their clan territory has been misunderstood. Although the chief would be dressed in silks and lace, with gold and silver accoutrements, his splendour reflected on the whole clan. They were his blood relatives. The oft-repeated notion that the clans arose through the process of people taking their name from some chief they decided to follow has no basis in fact. The clan system grew out of the earlier tribal system, the social cohesion of which was ultimately formed round the kin-relationship. The use of the standard term 'The MacIntosh' or 'The MacDonald' illustrates the reality. As head of the clan he represented all of its people, present, past and future, and it was a matter of pride for Highlanders to have their chief better dressed or turned out than the chiefs of other clans. The natural companions of the chief were not other chiefs, but his own people, among whom he was perceived to be the living representative of the original founder of the clan. Although his power was considerable, he was part of the clan, unlike the feudal kings who were considered to be above the entire population and answerable to God alone. Or at least this is what the feudal kings wanted people to think.

In clan society, the chief's power had limitations and these stretch back into the mists of time and were an inherent part of his role in clan, ie tribal society. Each warrior in these societies was essentially driven by his own sense of honour – the males all appear to have been raised to be warriors – and it was unthinkable that any warrior would follow a leader who was not worthy of his respect and loyalty. We know that those who might become chief had to lead raids in their youth to show their own skills and capacities, but in times of wholesale war, as opposed to the much more sporadic, if regular, raiding that took place between the tribes, the best warrior was the one who would be chosen to lead the clan's troops. This makes absolute sense. We are talking of people who are raised within societies where all around them are their kin with whom they share everything, though undoubtedly some were better off than others. Their interests were united behind the chief whose job was effectively to protect and advance those interests. Such societies had a certain level of equality amongst their members though they were certainly not democratic in the modern sense, although an early Roman writer did say the Picts did practise democracy, telling us, 'Their form of government is for the most part democratic, and they've a great liking for plunder.' (Dio 1927, LXXVI.12.1). There can be no doubt that there was a level of egalitarianism amongst the people of Scotland in general and amongst the Highland clans in particular.

A few examples should illustrate this. As early as the Battle of Mons Graupius c.80CE we have Tacitus putting these words in the mouth of Calgacus, the leader (not the King) of the Caledonians:

> Whenever I consider why we are fighting and how we have reached this crisis, I have a strong sense that this day of your splendid rally may mean the dawn of liberty for the whole of Britain. You have mustered to a man and to a man you are free... We, the last men on earth, the last of the free, have been shielded till today by he very remoteness and seclusion for which we are famed... Brigands of the world they have exhausted the land by their indiscriminate plunder, and now they ransack the sea... Robbery, butchery, rapine, the liars call Empire; they create a desolation and call it peace.
>
> Tacitus, 1948, p.79–80

This passage is perhaps nothing more than Agricola's son-in-law enhancing his reputation by presenting Calgacus as an honourable and worthy opponent, but it does strike a chord that echoes down the centuries.

Nearly 1,300 years later we have the remarkable Declaration of Arbroath in which the Scottish people give voice,

But at length it pleased God, who only can heal after
wounds, to restore us to liberty, from these innumerable
calamities, by our most serene prince, king and lord Robert,
who, from the delivering of his people and his own rightful
inheritance from the enemy's hand, did, like another Joshua
or Maccabeus, most cheerfully undergo all manner of toil,
fatigue, hardship and hazard. The Divine Providence, the
right of succession by the laws and customs of the kingdom
(which we will defend till death) and the due and lawful
consent and assent of all the people, made him our king and
prince. To him we are obliged and resolved to adhere in all
things, both upon the account of his right and his own
merit, as being the person who hath restored the people's
safety in defence of their liberties. But after all, if this prince
shall leave these principles he hath so nobly pursued, and
consent that we or our kingdom be subjected to the king or
people of England, we will immediately endeavour to expel
him, as our enemy and as the subverter both of his own and
our rights, and we will make another king, we will defend
our liberties; For so long as there shall be but one hundred
of us remain alive we will never consent to subject ourselves
to the dominion of the English. For it is not glory, it is not
riches, neither is it honours, but it is liberty alone that we
fight and contend for, which no honest man will lose but
with his life.

Adam, 1993 p.12

Both of these statements speak of a form of governance which is
anything but the despotic rule of a single individual. In the first
instance we are told that Calgacus is the leader of the massed
tribes, not their king or supreme chief, and a thousand years later,
in Christian Scotland, it is clear that even the king is answerable to
the people. He is the King of the Scots, not King of Scotland, a
distinction of great importance because it underlines the fact that
without the consent of the ruled there is no ruler. We cannot be

sure that Tacitus was doing anything other than presenting an idealised form of a suitable opponent in the panegyric to his father-in-law but it is remarkable that we have statements over such a period of time that have the same sense of egalitarianism.

Even in the latter, declining years of Highland Gaelic society, when most chiefs had accepted paper deeds for lands they and theirs had held for centuries, and were on the way to becoming that saddest of all social groups, the Lairds, sole owners of what had been the much-loved lands of entire societies, things were never as feudal or class-ridden as south of the border. Burt's *Letters From a Gentleman* written in the 1720s tells us about the Highlanders' relationship with their chief,

> ...and as the meanest among them pretend to be his Relations by Consanguinity, they insist upon the Privilege of taking him by the Hand whenever they meet him. Concerning this last, I once saw a Number of very discontented Countenances when a certain Lord, one of the Chiefs, endeavoured to evade this Ceremony. It was in Presence of an English Gentleman in high station, from whom he would have willingly have concealed the Knowledge of such seeming Familiarity with slaves of so wretched Appearance, and thinking it, I suppose, as a kind of Contradiction to what he had often boasted at other Times, viz., his despotic Power over his Clan.
>
> 1998, p.193

It is noticeable that he says that it is the member of the clan insisting on *his* right to shake his Chief's hand. While this does not mean that the two were absolute equals it does show that within the tribal/clan system there was a social system that was totally unlike that of England where there were aristocracy, gentry and, effectively, serfs, or as Burt puts it here – slaves. There is a level of egalitarianism that is the direct antithesis of feudalism. The supposed absolute power of the Scottish chief over his clansmen does not fit in with this eyewitness account. Another related instance occurred when a chief, educated and living away from the clan lands, on returning to take his place at the head of his clan, offended all those assumed to be his followers. This is how the situation was described by Logan in *The Scottish Gael*:

> The anecdote of the young chief of Clanranald is well known. On his return to take possession of his estate, observing the profuse quantity of cattle that had been slaughtered to celebrate his arrival, he very unfortunately remarked that a few hens might have answered the purpose. This exposure of a narrow mind, and inconsiderate display of indifference to the feeling of his people, were fatal.' We will have nothing to do with a hen chief,' said the indignant clansmen, and immediately raised one of his brothers to the dignity.
>
> Logan 1831, p.195

Part of the reaction to the 'Hen Chief's' ignorance and disdain of his own clan's traditions we can be pretty sure resulted from the fact that a feast greeting for a new chief would have been considered a momentous occasion in clan life, and the reason for a good party for the entire clan. The handing of power to his brother echoes ancient practice in Scotland where a brother was considered to be closer to the original founder of the clan than the chief's son, who was a further generation removed. This was perhaps the reason why Malcolm Canmore's sons succeeded each other to the throne in the 11th century. The clansfolk of the medieval period and later lived much as their remote ancestors in the Dark Ages did, living in the same glens, practising a form of subsistence agriculture, hunting, fishing and enjoying the occasional raid to lift others' cattle. Certainly by the medieval period they had become Christians, at least on the surface, and soon had access to more sophisticated weaponry in the form of firearms but there seems to be much in their way of life that was just the same as in Pictish times. In this regard we should remember that many of the clans claim descent from the Picts. In his book *The Scottish People*, James Rennie suggested that a considerable number of clans claimed Pictish origin including Brodie, Buchanan, Chisholm, Davidson, Dunbar, Farquharson, Forbes, Graham, Keith, Macbean, MacDuff, MacFarlane, MacKintosh, MacMillan, MacNaughton, MacPherson, Munro, Murray, Ogilvie, Robertson, Rose, Ross, Shaw, Skene, Sutherland and Urquhart (Rennie 1960). When one considers that other clans seem to have based their supposed genealogies on an Anglo–Norman origin out of a need to try and keep up with their English friends, it is obvious just how central the continuity from Pictish times was to late Highland society.

We should perhaps think of the tribes of Dark Age Scotland as extended families banding together with neighbours to form tribes within defined territories when necessary, but spending much of their lives living in small, scattered kin groups. The Romans again tell us they had no cities as such and the hilltop locations that we have been told are all forts were probably as much sacral sites as political or social centres.

Much has been made in British history of the influence of Rome but once again this pertains much more to England than to Scotland. The Romans were briefly in Scotland, even if their monumental building skills have left the walls they raised still visible in our landscape. The Antonine Wall has been shown to have been in use for little more than 20 years and had to be rebuilt at least once in that period (Swan 1999). The various lines of Roman forts in Scotland suggests that they were essentially supply lines. Again, much has been made of finds like the Roman silver on Traprain Law, an undoubted major site of the period. However, as AP Smyth points out in *Warlords and Holy Men* (1984, pp.40–41) there were many more Roman antiquities found in East Prussia, which the Romans never visited, than have ever been found in Scotland. Yes, they were here but, in historical terms, briefly indeed, and while they may have kept some influence over the lands adjoining Hadrian's Wall, between the Tyne and Tees there is no hard evidence to suggest that they had that much effect further north. 'They came, they seen, they went' as the poet Liz McNiven succinctly put it. (McHardy 2001, pp.55–6). This is of significance because in attempting to understand the symbols of the Picts many earlier writers have seen Roman influence as being extremely significant. I do not.

As far back as the 4th Millennium BCE the people in Scotland were carving cup-and-ring and spiral patterns on stones and raising sophisticated megalithic structures. They were not some poor ignorant savages waiting to be brought into the light by the civilising Romans, no matter how much this concept appealed to the Empire builders of 18th and 19th century Britain.

All of the early literary sources we have that mention Scotland in our period are written from an outside viewpoint. Even where sources like the Irish Annals might incorporate material that originated in communities such as Iona, these were essentially Christian, just as the Roman sources are essentially imperial. So, not only do we have no identifiable written sources from within Scotland, those that are contemporary are effectively second-hand. Early annal sources tell us little more than dates of significant battles or the deaths of those whom the annalists themselves considered important. As I hope to show that many of the non-Christian Pictish symbols are not only pagan, but can be seen as parts of a cohesive belief-system, it is clear that the literary sources will not be of much help. Just as in later periods, Scottish history has been skewed by an essentially Empire perspective so the earliest sources are overwhelmingly Christian. However, some early literary sources do point towards ideas and beliefs that can be seen as supportive of what I suggest.

Essentially, North Britain in the so-called Dark Ages – the name arising precisely from that lack of literary sources already alluded to – was a series of overlapping tribal warrior societies, with essentially self-sufficient economies, though evidence exists to show some long-term, long-distance trade in commodities such as the gold and amber mentioned. There was also trade with the Romans

in such things as bears and hunting dogs, though this is an area –
the economic history of early Scotland – where much work remains
to be done. The possibilities that the Romans might have been
trading for items like glass, coal and possibly metals such as lead
and silver is currently another area under consideration by
economic historians. Just because we are dealing with non-literate
tribal societies does not mean that we are dealing with people who
are either ignorant or unsophisticated. As has been noted, at least
some of the ancestors of the Picts had been part of the megalithic,
world and contacts over the North Sea had been continuous for
millennia. Also, although the focus of much male activity in such
societies was battle, this does not mean that they were constantly at
war. On the contrary it seems, from material as late as the 18th
century, that the inter-raiding between clans (tribes) was how the
warriors proved their skill and bravery and was an accepted and
regularised part of society (McHardy 2004, pp.3–31). In Galloway,
as late as the 17th century the autumnal moon of September and
October was known in south-west Scotland as 'MacLaren's Lantern'
from the regular incursions by that clan into the area. The focus of
such raids was usually to lift cattle – since the Iron Age cattle were
the prime symbol of wealth amongst the clans, as much in the
Borders and Galloway as in the Highlands till very late – and those
considered the most skilful appear to have been those who could
escape without the need for battle.

There were a great many rules and customs associated with
such 'creachs' as the raids were known, with arrangements of an
economic nature that could be made with those clans over whose
lands the cattle were taken home. When the raid did result in
violence the evidence shows that the ensuing battles were often
fought to a strict set of rules.

Probably the best-known instance of such rules of engagement is
the Battle of the Inch at Perth in 1396, when 30 men each from
two clans fought a pre-arranged battle. As late as the 18th century
in Angus there is an account of the inhabitants of Fearn in
Strathmore catching up with a bunch of caterans, or Highland

warriors, from Deeside, at the head of Glen Lethnot. Although the men from Fearn, on the northern rim of Strathmore, would be considered as Lowlanders by most standards, their leader agreed to settle the matter by single combat with the leader of the caterans (Ibid., pp.48–55). The agreement was that whoever won the swordfight would keep the cattle, horses etc. that had been 'lifted'. This was a mistake on the part of the Fearn men as the leader of the caterans was a man well over six feet tall with an enormous reach and no little skill with the sword. It was only when one of the caterans fired at a hare running between the two sides, believing it to be a witch, we are told, that open battle broke out and the heavily outnumbered Deeside men were all killed.

This type of behaviour is supported by many other instances and it seems likely that it was very ancient indeed and might well have been the norm amongst the tribal peoples of a millennium before, and possibly even earlier. All the evidence we have from Scotland and Ireland suggests a long-lived, cattle-rearing, warrior society. One of the aspects of this society was that there was always an elective aspect to the leadership and, given the close blood relationship between clan members, this can hardly be considered surprising.

I have already alluded to the practice of leadership in battle being given to the most capable and in 6th century Scotland this could explain what appears to have been happening amongst the British tribes of southern and central Scotland when the battle leader Arthur led a combined force of Christian tribes against a series of pagan sites, laying the basis for the growth of the legends of King Arthur in later years (McHardy 2001). As I have pointed out there, stories of King Arthur, and a considerable number of related place-names, survived in areas that are nowadays considered to have been Pictish, or as in the case of Scotland south of the Forth Clyde line, should be, certainly in the first half of the 1st Millennium.

This egalitarianism amongst such tribal warriors is supported by recent work on 'The Gododdin', the earliest surviving work in the P-Celtic language now known as Welsh. The poem is dated to the beginning of the 7th century and contains the earliest reference to Arthur as a great warrior. It is thought to have been written amongst the P-Celtic-speaking peoples of eastern Scotland, known as the Gododdin who appear in Ptolemy's 2nd century CE map as the Votadini. John T Koch suggests that previous interpretations that the disastrous battle raid that forms the subject of the work was led by a 'king' or chief called *Mynydawc Mwynvawr*, are simply wrong. He sees the relevant phrase as meaning something more like the 'luxurious mountain court or hall' (1997, p.xlvi) rather than being a personal name. Earlier historians, assuming the need for a king-like figure, saw what they wanted to see. This suggestion – of tribal warriors gathered together on a hilltop as opposed to a king organising, and perhaps paying for the raid – is supported in the text. Each of the 60 verses is concerned with one individual warrior. The raid was carried out by 300 warriors, but even if we have all of the original poem the fact that 60 of the warriors are mentioned makes it clear that they were all, if not equal, then of very similar status. None are given titles; the attributes mentioned are all to do with skill in battle and bravery. No one is described as the leader and there is no mention of them being followers. Even if the poem was initially longer and contained such material, the focus on one individual after another is strong evidence for the importance of these individuals in their own right, as part of the group, rather than as part of the following of some other individual.

The Gododdin were direct neighbours of the Picts and at least one Pictish Symbol Stone was found close to one of their major sites, Edinburgh Castle Rock. Like the Picts, they were a P-Celtic-speaking, tribal warrior society and just as these tribal peoples seem to have shared Arthurian traditions it is likely that their pre-Christian religion was also similar, if not exactly the same. As Celtic-speaking, pastoralist, warrior societies they certainly had much in common. In the west of Scotland at this time, the Britons of Strathclyde formed the same kind of society, the main difference between them and the Gaelic(Q-Celtic)-speaking tribes of Dalriada to their north-west being language, though their tongues shared many aspects, particularly in the description of landscape. And, as I have stated, from the Roman perspective they all seem to have been Picts and I would suggest that they were united, not only by language and socio-economic structure, but also by ritual and belief patterns.

I have suggested (McHardy 2001) that the original 'King' Arthur was leading a Christian crusade against either pagans, or possibly against the apostate Picts who are mentioned by Bede (1955). This suggests that some areas of Pictland had been Christianised at an earlier period and then lapsed back into paganism. Whatever the actual situation, and it is unlikely we will ever understand it fully, there is little doubt that there were ongoing times of significant tension between Christian and pagan. The martyrdom of such saints as Constantine in Kintyre and Donnan on the island of Eigg in the 6th and 8th centuries are examples.

In *The Quest for Arthur* (2001) I put forward the idea that Scotland remained essentially tribal till at least the 7th century when the combination of Northumbrian expansionism and the centralising tendencies of the Christian church began to push the tribes into more centralised and structured polities that eventually grew into kingdoms. Sources from the later Dark Ages and the Early Medieval periods, understandably interpreted these earlier periods in terms of what they themselves knew, but I suggest that talk of kingdoms is anachronistic before the late 7th century, at the earliest. It is from what I perceive of as these linked series of pagan tribal societies that the meanings here suggested for the Pictish Symbol Stones arise.

CHAPTER TWO

Pictish Symbolism

THE BEAUTIFUL SYMBOLS from the art we think of as Celtic and Pictish developed from a continuum of society that stretches back millennia. Much of what is generally seen as Celtic Art, the Book of Kells for instance, in fact owes a great debt to the art of the Picts, as modern research tells us that this great illuminated text, started on the holy island of Iona before being taken to Kells in Ireland, was heavily influenced by Pictish art (Henderson, 1982). It may even have been started by artists trained in the Pictish tradition.

Since the publication of *The Early Christian Monuments of Scotland* (ECMS) by Allen and Anderson in 1903, the Pictish symbol stones have been accepted as falling into three main classes: Class I stones are those with simply picked out symbols, usually paired, on one side of rough, undressed stones, some, or perhaps even all, of which could have been standing stones from an earlier time; Class II stones, often shaped, have Class I symbols on one side and ornate Christian crosses on the other side, sometimes with clearly pagan symbols alongside them and combine the earlier picking out with some relief sculpture; Class III stones are later, beautifully shaped with ornate crosses on one side and various Biblical or hunting scenes on the other and some involve highly complex relief carving. In this work, I shall be concentrating on the symbols that occur on the Class I stones.

Nowadays we can discern different schools of Pictish art in the later Class II and Class III periods, and by the time the Book of Kells was started, some of these schools had possibly been in existence for generations. Because we have virtually no written records from the Picts themselves, their art has been the focus of much speculation and study over the past few centuries. Much of this interest has focused on the Christian iconography that is so obvious on the Class II and Class III stones, some of which, like the Hilton of Cadboll or Shandwick Stones, are truly magnificent and whose universal significance in the history of art is still under-appreciated. However, on both the Class I and Class II stones, we see symbols that survive from pagan times which laid the basis for the later flowering of Pictish art. Briefly, The combination of both pagan and Christian symbols on Class II stones and the coexistence of relief and incised carving suggest a considerable level of continuity. The earlier symbols from the pre-Christian period in combination with clear Pictish iconography could simply be part of the process of assimilation carried on by the Christian church. In 601CE, Pope Gregory, in a letter to Abbot Mellitus talking about pagan temples, actually stipulates,

> If the temples are well built, they are to be purified from devil-worship, and dedicated to the service of the one true God. In this way, we hope that the people, seeing that its temples are not destroyed, may abandon idolatry and resort to these places as before, and may come to know and adore the one true God.
>
> Bede, 1, 30, p.86

Although this letter applies specifically to England, there is no reason to doubt the same process would have been common in Scotland. This could account for the continuing existence of pre-Christian symbols on the Class II stones – they were intended to provide something familiar for converts within the context of the new religion. As we shall see, the taking over of pre-Christian sites may well have led to the still visible existence of churches on mounds in the Scottish landscape. Another possibility, especially if the stones were used as teaching aids for preaching, perhaps in both pre-Christian and Christian circumstances, is that there was some period of ongoing contemporary pagan and Christian use. This is not something we would expect the church, once it had become dominant, to let us know about. We know that at least as late as the 18th century there were pagan practices, like bull sacrifice continuing in parts of Scotland (McNeill 1957, p.29) so the likelihood of a complete and overwhelming changeover from earlier religion to Christianity is not perhaps that likely, despite what we have been told. Many Pictish Symbol Stones have in fact been found in kirkyards or close by, and this, in the case of the Class I and II stones, could be as a direct result of the early church taking over previously sacred sites. The problem has always been that the Class I symbols have been seen as indecipherable. I do not believe this to be the case. Brodie (1996), commenting on the finding of so many Pictish stones at or near church sites gives the following:

> As it seems unlikely that stones used only for utilitarian purposes, e.g. boundary markers, etc., would be gathered together in such a manner, it is difficult not to conclude that symbol stones had a primary function relating to the worship of pagan gods.
>
> 1996, p.21

Brodie sees the symbols as having a direct relationship to ideas of fertility which certainly makes sense in terms of what will here be presented in terms of pre-Christian belief.

Many of the 'enigmatic' symbols on the Class II stones in particular can be traced back to early Christian bestiaries and other religious texts [FIG. 2]. This reinforces the idea that it is likely that the Class I stones were already sacred symbols in their own right before the carvings were added, and that the symbols themselves had some sort of sacral significance. In the past it was thought that the use of simple incision was restricted to the early stones and that the later stones used the more sophisticated relief sculpture. However, although simple incision does seem to be the earliest technique, it continued to be used by the Pictish sculptors alongside relief sculpture till a relatively late period.

FIG. 2
Glamis Manse

Many commentators (Cummins (1999), Jackson (1993), Samson (1992)) have analysed the symbols, and their groupings, on the basis that they are memorial stones. There is no absolute proof of this and the anachronistic comparisons with later feudal heraldic practices ignore the realities of contemporary society. Before the growth of Northumbria in the 7th century, we have no proof of anything like kingdoms existing in what we now call Scotland. The tribal systems of the native peoples lasted into the 15th and 16th centuries in Galloway and the Borders while the Highland clan system did not entirely disappear till the mid-18th century. The idea that the Pictish Symbol Stones were memorials to aristocratic members of contemporary Pictish societies seems unlikely in such societies. Tribes are aggregations of family groupings – often as in the case of the Highland clans, or their Border counterparts, sharing a common name. This common name is generally that of a distant ancestor from whom all claim ultimate descent, though the chief is generally the most direct descendant – and this is what creates his position at the centre of the tribe. These tribal societies lived in small, scattered groupings – the Romans tell us they had no cities or towns – with each group forming a small part of a greater tribe. While the chief is absolutely central to the functioning of such societies, it is the role of the chief and not the individual that is important. As has been noted by various writers, Burt (1998), Skene (1837), Scott et al (1843), the chiefs themselves could be removed from their position at the head of the clan if their behaviour was considered unsatisfactory.

If the stones were raised to particular chiefs then there should surely be many more of them and we should see what amounts to series of them, ie cemeteries akin to the series of burial mounds found in Scandinavia. There are not even one or two groupings utilising the same symbols close enough to each other to suggest they were erected by the same tribe. Samson (1992) and more recently Cummins (2009) have analysed the symbols as referring directly to named individuals but this depends on the assumption that the stones themselves were memorials to specific individuals. The idea that they could be raised to kings is, I believe, anachronistic, certainly in terms of the Class I stones. The lack of significant numbers of them, or any specific historical, folklore or archaeological evidence linking any one of the stones to a named individual is striking. If one chief within a clan system, where all around him were his relatives, had a stone raised in his memory, we would expect his successors to want the same. In the closest contemporary literary source we have, the 7th century battle poem 'The Gododdin', we have seen each verse is dedicated to one warrior, none of whom are given hierarchic status – what matters is their bravery and skill as a warrior.

Jackson (1984) suggested that there were strong components of dynastic arrangements shown on the stones. His complex argument is to some extent based on the number of different symbols. We cannot be sure that all the Pictish stones have survived, therefore building any theoretical construct on the extant symbols is fraught with problems. There may well have been other symbols. Also his reliance on the pairing of symbols ignores those which do not conform to his theory.

As for the idea of commemorating a single named individual, there is one main problem. Given the scattered nature of the surviving Pictish Symbol Stones, with some of them coming in distinct localised groups, there are simply not enough of them. If there was one inter-tribal marriage that required the raising of a symbol stone, we should expect others. Although we cannot be sure, there were not many more Symbol Stones in the landscape, it seems dubious to argue from the lack of evidence that there must have been many more. The idea of a memorial on a grave is hard to locate before the coming of Christianity though it is a distinct possibility that Class III stones had a personalised component within their creation. However, the Class I stones cannot with any certainty be linked to individuals. It is perhaps salutary that we have learned from archaeology that the prehistoric chambered cairns were communal graves and not, as was previously supposed, memorials to 'great' individuals. In short, I would suggest the Class I, and probably also the Class II, stones in no way represent individual burials or commemorations.

Recently, there has been a series of articles on trying to decipher the symbols as some sort of alphabet. As yet, I have seen nothing that convinces me that this is anything other than an academic exercise, and one I suspect with little likelihood of ever amounting to much.

Many past commentators on the art of the Picts have stressed the influence of external peoples such as the Romans, the Northumbrians and of course the Irish. While there are clear dateable influences in Class II and Class III stones in such iconography as that of King David and the fantastic animals from bestiaries, there is no reason to seek outside influence for the earliest symbols with which we are primarily concerned here. As far back as the Stone Age, stones were being carved in Scotland and elsewhere in the British Isles, mainly with cup-and-ring and spiral motifs but, as Dr Isabel Henderson has pointed out, many of the most obviously Pictish of our symbols show strong similarities to what she has called Eurasian hunter art. From the British Isles to Siberia, and as far south as the Black Sea, there are recurring motifs and similarities of styles which are probably due to the fact that so many of these societies had similar lifestyles, similar technologies and even similar beliefs as late as the 1st Millennium CE. I have looked at this further in *The Quest for the Nine Maidens* (McHardy 2003). And as we shall see, representational art does seem to have a long history in Scottish rock carving.

The interpretation of the symbols here presented is to a considerable extent based on surviving early written material in Welsh and Irish traditions. Much of this material survives in texts from the medieval period but there is little doubt that the stories themselves originally came from older oral tradition. Modern scholarship has shown that oral transmission can carry accurate, provable, data over thousands of years (Isaacs 1991 *passim*) and in combination with other disciplines, the study of such legendary and mythological material can help us gain a clearer picture of the past. What has survived within Welsh sources is at the least descended from the traditionary material of people speaking P-Celtic languages well beyond what we nowadays call Wales. The Picts are believed to have spoken a P-Celtic language. Material like 'The Gododdin', the earliest extant Welsh poem, is known to have been written near Edinburgh in the early 7th century, when the dominant language in the Lothians, and much of the rest of Scotland, was the P-Celtic Neo-Archaic North Brythonnic, a language that was the ancestor of modern Welsh (and a bit of a mouthful). As the Welsh language went into retreat it took with it mythological and legendary material that had at an earlier time been known over much of Britain. As it is generally accepted that the Picts were predominantly a P-Celtic-speaking people and given the fact that we have Arthurian stories and place-names in various parts of what was the land of the Picts, it is relatively certain that they would have had much in common with the other P-Celtic tribes and peoples in terms of their culture. The tenacity of oral transmission even in supposedly literate society is remarkable. In the 1980s a new version of the Voyage of St Brendan was collected in Scotland from a member of a travelling family, none of whose ancestors had been literate (Douglas 1987, p.55f.). The assumption on the part of so many scholars that once literacy is introduced oral transmission disappears, is simply wrong. A large amount of early Welsh material concerns the *Gwr Y Gogledd*, the Men of the North and refers to the heroic traditions of the P-Celtic-speaking peoples of Strathclyde and Lothian. It is also note-worthy that there are a considerable number of references to *Prydain* in The Mabinogion, The Welsh Triads etc, where the term is speci-fically applied to the land of the Picts. This term *Prydain*, initially meaning 'Pictland', could of course be the root of the term Britain itself. While much of the material surviving in Welsh was once known over a much wider area than Wales, some such material survived language shift and continued to be told in their traditional areas – again the Scottish Arthurian material is a prime example. The story from Meigle (McHardy 2005, p.133f.) might have originated in a P-Celtic form, moved into Q-Celtic Gaelic and survived till recently in the Germanic–Scots tongue. The suggestion that Dark Age Scotland was not formed of ethnically discrete, monoglot cultures would make this more feasible.

One of the confusing aspects of trying to discern settlement and language patterns in Dark Age Scotland is language itself. We are used to thinking of Scotland as having been totally Gaelicised in the Early Medieval period but this is not necessarily so. Some scholars believe there could have been remnants of P-Celtic speakers in Scotland as late as the 11th century. However, what is known is that there are a great many place-name terms that are cognate in Welsh and Gaelic. If the Picts were P-Celtic speakers and had a language similar to their neighbours in Lothian and Strathclyde, then perhaps in areas like Angus, Fife and even the Lothians we have remnants of originally Pictish terminology for the landscape that has been interpreted, in good faith, as having been Gaelic. Much of the place-name evidence scholars rely on was compiled by Ordnance Survey inspectors, few of whom had much knowledge of any of the Celtic languages. This is merely to underline the fact that in the Dark Age period, things were perhaps more fluid than has generally been considered, and that the inter-relationship between the different tribal groupings was considerably more extensive than those scholars relying on defining people by the language they spoke have to date appreciated. New ideas such as those being developed by Win Scutt (Scutt URL) concerning the pre-Roman existence of Germanic-speaking peoples in England clearly have a bearing on what may have been the situation in Scotland. This idea was mooted in the 1940s by Fowler in his *False Foundations of British History* and the ramifications of this in combination with the genetic research of Oppenheimer and others means that the picture we have of pre-Roman Britain is in flux. In the light of this, the long-rejected idea put forward by John Jamieson in his *A Dissertation on the Origins of the Scots Language,* which was a preface to his *Dictionary of the Scottish Language,* that the Picts spoke an early form of Scots, is perhaps worth revisiting.

The links between Scotland and Ireland have been continuous since the Stone Age and in Pictish times some of the Scottish population, the Scots of Dalriada. shared a language with, and had close ties to the population of at least the northern part of Ireland. This means that the peoples of Ireland, western Scotland and the Hebrides were in regular mutual contact with consequent implications for trade, inter-marriage and cultural interaction. Likewise, contact with northern Europe can be traced back through prehistory.

CHAPTER THREE

Dating

IT HAS GENERALLY been accepted that the Pictish Symbol Stones started being carved in the 6th century, or possibly slightly earlier. This assumption is based on the belief that the Picts started carving animal and geometric symbols as a result of outside influence in the Roman and post-Roman period. The truth is that although we can date the Class II and Class III stones with some accuracy on art historic grounds, we have no real idea as to the date of the Class I stones. With most recent Pictish archaeology concentrating on Christian sites such as cemeteries and monasteries, we have no recent data that could help us date these earlier stones. I suggest that the beliefs underpinning the symbols on these stones are part of a continuum that stretches back to the far past and we can see similarities with some art styles from the Iron Age and even earlier. I would therefore propose that the Class I stones are potentially much earlier. We must await further archaeological investigation, accidental or otherwise, before we can hope to resolve this further. The Collessie Man [FIG. 3] is a reasonable match for the description of

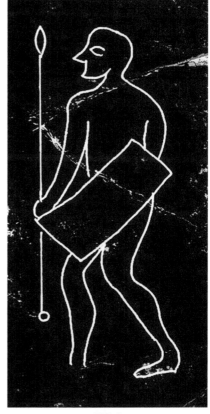

FIG. 3
Collessie Man

indigenous warriors given by Dio Cassius writing in the early years of the 3rd century CE and, given the existence of carved deer from a much earlier period, it seems there are grounds for thinking that the symbols may be of earlier provenance. It may be conceivable that carving symbols on standing stones did not occur before the arrival of the Romans and the Christian church but the carving of deer in bedrock at Ballochmyle (Ballochmyle URL) and Glen Domhain (GlenDomhain URL) suggests that the ideas underlying the Pictish Symbols may well be rooted in much earlier times. A similar carving to the Glen Domhain was discovered a few years ago on Blackford Hill in Edinburgh (Blackford Hill URL).

CHAPTER FOUR

Symbolism

SYMBOLS IN PRE-LITERATE societies potentially contain many meanings at once, and we will probably never know the full range of meanings of the beautiful and intricate designs our ancestors took so much time, and care, to create. When we see these symbols from the distant pagan past or from the early years of Christianity in Scotland we are looking at art that is highly stylised – telling of long term development – magnificently executed and infused with a sense of wonder and sanctity. Some of the symbols can be linked to the great mythological tales of the Celtic- and perhaps Germanic-speaking tribes that inhabited this land. Such tales as those of the great hero Arthur told among the Brythonnic-speaking peoples who lived during the Dark Ages in what we call Scotland find echo in the Gaelic tales of Finn MacCoul amongst the Gaelic speakers of Scotland and Ireland. Other motifs used by the Picts have much in common with the mythology of the Nordic peoples, who have played such an important part in our nation's history and development. Yet other symbols reflect usages of earlier times in different parts of Europe and where we can tell anything of their meaning it always seems essentially spiritual. While we tend to see all of pre-Christian Europe as pagan, this covers a multitude of differences and divergences among the peoples of our Continent. What we can be sure of is that they believed in many gods and goddesses and there is evidence that a major Mother Goddess figure was common to many societies over many, many centuries.

Symbolism among peoples who have no written language is generally extremely complex and related to the tales and traditions of their culture that are passed from generation to generation by the spoken word. In pre-literate societies all knowledge must be passed on in this way. In addition to their primary meaning, symbols can have further, hidden meanings, obvious only to those who have been initiated into the mysteries and rituals of their own society. It is impossible for people in our modern world to ever understand all the possible meanings of any symbol, or group of symbols as the knowledge underpinning them has survived patchily. Today we tend to see symbols like direction signs on motorways, radiation and electricity symbols to warn us of danger, or simply to direct us to gender specific toilet facilities. Such a reduction of the inherent capacity of symbols to contain multi-faceted meanings is the direct antithesis of how symbols work in societies lacking written literature.

We can, however, see some of the meanings inherent in earlier symbols and link them to known traditions and patterns of belief and possibly even ritual. Modern scholarship has consistently underestimated the sophistication of pre-literate peoples, shackled as we now are to the written word but, as research in Australia has shown, (Isaacs, 1991) there is a capacity for oral transmission to handle specific information accurately over thousands of years. What is clear is that however much we can understand of any symbol or group of related symbols, there will always be meanings that lie beyond our understanding and knowledge. A simple circle, after all, can represent the sun, the moon, the turning of the seasons, time itself, a cauldron and perhaps even the journey through life and death. Sometimes such multi-faceted symbols can be further related to specific beliefs and various figures in the pagan pantheon. In terms of such pre-literate symbolism the more you know, the more complex a symbol can become and the more meanings it can be seen to contain. The people who created these generally beautiful symbols were not psychologically much different from us and they too lived in families, within communities that likely thought of themselves as modern, at least in the sense that they were the living contemporary representatives of a culture that they had inherited from generations of their ancestors.

By considering the myth and folklore of the tribal peoples of

Scotland, the British Isles and nearby Continental Europe, and drawing upon the analysis of Ancient European symbolism developed by such scholars as Marija Gimbutas (in her seminal *Goddesses and Gods of Ancient Europe* (1982)) this book gives suggestions of various meanings to the symbols herein treated. Much will be said about the Mother Goddess – a figure of considerable importance in the pre-Christian world. Little is made of the standard historical approach of analysing artefacts according to their assumed masculine, militaristic and aristocratic importance – as if the history of people on this planet concerns one sex only. I have not looked at every single one of the symbols used on the Class I stones in depth, but hopefully my analyses can be developed further.

CHAPTER FIVE

Before Literature

IT IS NOW accepted that societies that never knew literacy have
passed accurate knowledge over many thousands of years. Western
educated people used to think that tales of giant wombats and
kangaroos were fantasy till bones of such animals were found from
a period not long after the first humans settled Australia. Jane
Isaacs in her book *Australian Dreaming* (1991 p.15) tells of the
bones of such creatures, now known as Diprodotons, being found
near Melbourne alongside an early human campsite and dated to
over 30,000 years ago. Without literacy, the indigenous peoples
kept alive knowledge of these animals now known to have been
extinct for 15,000 years. The use of paintings containing symbols
and stylised representations of places and animals is a central part
of Australian indigenous culture and doubtless helped in the
memory and transmission of much of the oral tradition. It seems
entirely likely that the earliest Class I Pictish stones could have been
utilised by Pictish tradition-bearers telling stories from their own
belief systems, while the later Christian stones could have been used
to tell Bible stories in a not dissimilar way. The depiction of specific
Biblical scenes on the Class II stones can be seen as confirming this
idea if we accept that the stones themselves have a provenance that
begins in pre-Christian times.

By focusing when possible on the mythological and legendary
material that has survived from Celtic and Germanic sources and
through comparison with other, mainly European symbol usage, it
is hoped this book will give some idea of the complex concepts that
lay behind these symbols and stories. The people who created this
great art were in many ways like ourselves – they lived and died,
loved and married, worked and sang and faced the daily challenges
of an uncertain world – just as we do. In their art we can still sense

the emotions and feelings of the artists and hopefully, as we understand more of their symbolism and meaning we can build upon what we learn to have a greater understanding of the ideas and beliefs that drove them. Today, as more and more people, including many artists, draw inspiration from Pictish art, we are perhaps now closer to seeing how we ourselves are linked with our ancient artist ancestors.

Over centuries and millennia beliefs alter, religions rise and fall and eventually disappear but these symbols are a reflection of a continuum as yet unbroken – the continuum of human life. Just as the symbols themselves have probably changed their meaning over such time, so today we too can infuse them with even more meaning. Today many of us think of ourselves as Scottish, even within the British state. The ancient Celtic-speaking tribes of Britain had no concept at all of the nation state – but we use symbols, just as they did. What is a flag if not a symbol? In one sense as long as the symbols mean something to someone, they are alive, even if the inherent meaning changes. What we can say is that the more we are aware of what the artist's meaning was, the more likely it is that new meanings will be a development in the continuum of a culture that first arose in the far past.

CHAPTER SIX

The Symbol Stones

ONE SUGGESTION FOR the use of the Class II and III symbol stones has been as 'texts' for Christian priests, perhaps following their pagan forerunners, to use in preaching. This makes sense, and raises the intriguing possibility that some of the Class II stones were in simultaneous use by both Christian and pagan priests. From Bede we know that it was official Christian policy to take over pagan temples to preach the Gospel. There are many churches in Scotland that seem to have been built on raised mounds that were already sacred sites, without necessarily having built structures. Logan (1831, p.214) notes that many churches have such mounds close by. The taking over of 'pagan precincts' could well account for the fact that so many of the Pictish Symbol Stones have been found in or adjoining kirkyards. The Aberlemno roadside stones include two Class I stones and one Class II stone and Doug Scott has noted that these stones form a midwinter sun alignment dating from c.2000BCE (Scott 2001, no. 61). Raising a church near what appears to be a pre-Christian sacred site would conform exactly to the process outlined by Pope Gregory to Bishop Mellitus, with the alignment perhaps being Christianised by the erections or alteration of the Class II stone here. Another such stone, to which we will return, is the Glamis Manse stone. On the cross side of this magnificent monument there are a series of symbols which I will suggest link directly back to pagan beliefs, and which might even suggest a direct continuity from pagan to Christian belief. Many commentators have noticed that many of the great Christian public fiestas of Mediterranean Europe contain obviously pagan motifs. Again this would correspond to the process suggested by Pope Gregory with certain aspects of ritual behaviour being absorbed into Christian behaviour to provide continuity with past practice.

In Scotland, the Reformation saw the destruction of much early material because it was considered to be 'Popish' and in this light it is remarkable that so many of the Pictish Symbol Stones survived.

The analysis here of the early symbols of the Picts is predicated on the assumption that the 'pagan' religion practised by the Picts would have been similar to that practised by their neighbours in England, Wales, Ireland and probably Scandinavia. I have drawn extensively on early Welsh and Irish texts to investigate these symbols. In the case of the Welsh texts, as I have argued regarding Arthurian material, the survival of that language at some distance from modern Scotland does not preclude the likelihood that much of the material that survives in Early Welsh was originally common to all of the P-Celtic-speaking tribes of Early Britain.

Animals

The use of animals in Insular Celtic Art is often complex and highly formalised. The Class i stones often show animals drawn directly and accurately from life. Unlike the geometric shapes they are clear representations of living creatures in the environment. Although the later stones often have mythical or composite animal forms, the early, purely pagan stones are often noteworthy for the beauty of the animal symbols – obviously drawn from living creatures and suggesting an identification with the animals and the environment that is total. Many of these animals find echo in the tales and traditions of the Celtic-speaking tribes of the British Isles and can be directly linked to mythological and legendary figures.

The art of the stones appears to us as having erupted fully formed on the Symbol Stones but this is probably due to no more than the lack of survival of other uses of this art (e.g. on wood, leather and metal). It also seems probable that many of the undressed slabs we think of as Class i Symbol Stones had an earlier function as standing stones, and though we cannot discern the exact meaning of such artefacts, a sacral function of some sort seems likely. Sadly, in today's increasingly polluted world the effects of acid rain and other substances are taking a heavy toll on those Pictish Symbol Stones which still survive in our landscape. Often the only solution is to take these magnificent works of art indoors where their beauty and glory can hopefully be preserved and appreciated.

Bear

Various people have put forward the suggestion that the much-faded symbol on the Keillor Stone is a bear [FIG. 4]. Although we know of no other stones with bears on them, we do know that

FIG. 4
Keillor Stone

bears were indigenous to Scotland in the 1st Millennium. Bears were associated with warriors in many societies and there is a suggested link between the figure of Arthur and the Bear. As I have argued earlier, Arthur was part of the common cultural inheritance of the P-Celtic language speaking societies and tales of him were probably common amongst the Picts.

Various scholars have noticed that there appears to be a link between the bear and the figure of Arthur. The following is from the Britannia website:

The name Arthur itself appears to derive from the Celtic word *Art*, meaning 'bear'. Could Arthur, like so many other Celtic gods, be merely a personification of the many revered animals of the wild? Later to become humanized like Loucetios, one of several Celtic deities known to be able to transform themselves into birds or beasts of the forest. Many such gods had stellar associations and the constellation of *Ursa Major* or the Great Bear is sometimes known as *Arthur's Wain* even today.

Three Bear-gods are known from the Celtic world. Strangely, they acted as both champion of bear-hunters and protectors of the beast itself. The most celebrated was, perhaps, *Artio*, worshipped near Berne in Switzerland and around Trier in Germany; but she was actually a goddess.

Britannia URL

Apart from the link here to a goddess figure, it is of interest that there is reference to shape-shifting, something which we will see in relation to other animals used as Pictish symbols.

Boar/Sow

Pigs have been associated with fertility and the feminine for a very long time, as was noted by Brown in the journal Folklore.

> The earliest record of a religious pig-cult is in the remains of cavemen in Palestine who can be traced from about 12,000 BCE to 1200 BCE. These remains prove that they worshipped a Mother Goddess to whom blood libations were poured into channels cut in the rock.
>
> Brown 1965, p.288

The only complete Class 1 boar we have is from Knocknagael, Inverness-shire [FIG. 5] though there is another faded boar on Dunadd, the capital of the Scottish Dalriada. [FIG. 6] Again this scarcity may be accidental, there may well have been more stones with boars on them in the past. Some people see the Keillor Stone as having a boar rather than a bear on it. The boar is, like the bull, often portrayed as a particularly masculine symbol – its ferocious-ness and utter lack of fear being seen as ideal attributes for a warrior. In many different societies the boar has been found on pieces of protective armour, shields etc, illustrating its attraction for the warrior.

In both Gaelic and Welsh mythology boars figure strongly. In *The Mabinogion* (Jones & Jones 1993, p.98f.) we are told that pigs originally came to Wales as a gift to the king Pwyll from Arawn, King of Annwn, the Underworld, underlining their magical

FIG. 5
Knocknagael

FIG. 6
Dunadd

properties. In the Mabinogion tale of *Culhwch and Olwen*, the hero, Culhwch, as part of a quest, had to retrieve a magic comb and scissors from between the ears of *Twrch Trwyth*, a great boar that was devastating Ireland. The comb and scissors were needed to dress the hair of the giant Ysbadden. Culhwch was assisted in his task by King Arthur and his men. The boar came to Wales and killed many of Arthur's men and laid waste to the countryside of Wales, Cornwall and Devon before the comb and scissors were taken. After this the great boar disappeared into the sea.

The great Gaelic hero, Finn MacCoul, in the only instance of unheroic behaviour told of him, had Diarmaid, his wife's lover, measure the length of the magic boar of Ben Gulbain by walking barefoot along its back. This led to one of the poisoned spines of the boar piercing Diarmaid's foot and Finn's reluctance to use his own magic to save him resulted in Diarmaid's death. In some versions of this tale, the boar is in fact the leader of a herd of swine kept by the *Mala Liath*, an old woman who is clearly a version of the Cailleach, and many warriors had died in hunting the beast. Diarmaid, in hunting the boar, throws the *Mala Liath* over a cliff when she tries to hinder him. DA Mackenzie thought that this tale contained memories of human sacrifice (1935, p.149) which may seem a bit far-fetched but Diarmaid's assault on the *Mala Liath* can be seen as a slight on the Old Religion.

It is worth noting that Ben Gulbain, where this latter tale is set, is not one place but several, in both Scotland and Ireland. This, I believe, is because the legends and myths of pre-literate society could only have meaning to their audience if they were presented within an environment familiar to that audience. This would also be the reason that Arthurian stories exist locally almost the length and breadth of what were the Brythonnic language speaking areas of Britain. If Ewan Campbell (2001) is correct, and his reasoning seems sound to me, and the polity of Dalriada was not founded from Ulster in the 6th century, Finn MacCoul can be understood to be as indigenous among the Gaelic-speaking peoples of Scotland as those of Ireland.

Saint Kentigern, patron saint of Glasgow, who came from British Strathclyde, spent some time in exile in Wales. He is said to have been the grandson of the mythical King Lot of the Lothians and great-nephew of Arthur, and is clearly a figure from British myth and legend who was taken over by the Christian church. He was associated with a white boar which led him to the place where he raised his church in Wales. The boar not only led him there but made it clear what had to be done. The following is from *The Lives of St Ninian and Kentigern*:

> Then they came to the place which the Lord had predestined for them the boar halted, and frequently striking the ground with his foot, and making a gesture of tearing up the soil of a little hill that was there with his long tusk, shaking his head repeatedly and grunting, he clearly showed to all that that was the place designed and prepared by God.
>
> Forbes 1874, p.76

We know that it was the specific policy of the Christian church to re-utilise already sacred places and in this tale we are perhaps seeing the boar, as a symbol or representative of paganism helping set up such a foundation for the new religion.

Mackenzie (1935, p.61) suggests that the Knocknagael boar 'was connected with the Orc (boar) clan of the Picts' after whom it has been suggested the Orkneys were named.

There is another significant carved boar in Scotland, though outside what has generally been considered to be under Pictish control. This is the boar carved on the flat surface on the hill-fort of Dunadd, in the Kilmartin valley, itself full of ancient monuments from the Stone Age onwards. This fort was the ancient capital of the Dalriadic Scots. Why should a Pictish type symbol be found in this important Scottish site? Perhaps the notion of the absolute separation of these peoples along linguistic lines is wrong. Perhaps again it was carved as a result of some sort of inter-tribal alliance between the Picts and Scots – the problem is that we have as yet no definite way of dating when rock surfaces were carved. I have stated (McHardy 2010) that from the Roman perspective I believe all the tribes of what we now call Scotland were Picts and the evidence from Irish Annals suggests that they were inter-related in some way. What we can be sure of is that the symbol of the boar was obviously significant to all of the early P- and Q-Celtic speakers of Dark Age Scotland and this importance stems from the pre-Christian period, and can be seen as an integral part of pagan belief. The boar however is also important in the beliefs of those other Pictish neighbours, the Norsemen. Although we have no specific records of Viking intrusion before the dawning of the 8th century there had been contact between the north of Britain and what we now think of as Scandinavia since at least Megalithic times. The development of Continental type timber halls shown by the excavations at Balbridie and elsewhere show that there was at the very least cultural contact across the North Sea long before the Pictish era. HRE Davidson tells us that, in *Norse Mythology*

The boar was associated with the goddess Freyja... It has generally been assumed that the choice of a pig as a symbol of the fertility goddess was due to its capacity for breeding but ... Peter Reynolds in his study of Iron Age agriculture (Reynolds, 1979:53) refers to the pig as a potential plough... Wild pigs have very long snouts, and their capacity to turn over the soil while searching for acorns might at least partly

account for their association with the goddess in both
Greece and northern Europe.

1998, p.64

We have here a symbol that possibly arises from direct observation
of the activity of the animal chosen to be the symbol.

Elsewhere, Davidson informs us,

> The realm of blackness was the underworld and the boar could
> carry the goddess Fryja there when she wanted to gain special
> knowledge, as we learn from the poem Hyundliljod in the
> poetic Edda, here her human lover Ottar takes on the form
> of a boar so that she can take him down to learn the names
> of his ancestors. After discovering his genealogy. Ottar drank
> the ale of remembrance, which may imply a link between the
> boar and the *minni* drunk at the fast in honour of dead
> ancestors, and thus with the Vanir deities also. In his rapid
> journey through the sky into the lower world, the boar shining
> so brilliantly must surely be a symbol of the travelling sun.

1988, p.50

Here we have a complicated series of relationships between the
boar and the goddess, the boar and the ancestors and the boar and
the sun. When we add in the widespread use of boar decoration in
battledress and weaponry we can clearly see the multivalent aspects
of one single symbol in pre-literate societies. What is clear is that
the pig has strong associations with both fertility in general and
goddesses in particular amongst various of the societies
neighbouring the Picts.

While the boar is seen as predominantly masculine and a symbol
of courage and ferocity, the sow is equally ferocious, particularly if
defending her young. One of these beasts, from Welsh tradition, is
Henwen, a great sow which is clearly a fertility symbol in its own
right. This is from the collection of Welsh Triads as given in Rhys's
Celtic Folklore;

Now one of the swine was with young and Henwen was her name; and it was foretold that the Isle of Prydain would be the worse for her litter; and Arthur collected the host of Prydain and went about to destroy it. Then one sow went burrowing and at the Headland of Hawstin in Kernyw she took to the sea with the swineherd following her. And in Maes Gwenith in Gwent she dropped a grain of wheat and a bee, and ever since Maes Gwenith is the best place for wheat and bees. And at Llonyon in Penfro she dropped a grain of barley and another of wheat; therefore the barley of Llonyon has passed into a proverb.

vol 2, p.504

Henwen is also said to have dropped various animals who caused devastation but the reference to wheat, bees and barley all point to her being a female symbol of fertility. I have already mentioned the location of legendary material within the known environment of the audience, or perhaps the territory of the tribes or peoples among whom the story was told. Here we have this happening in Prydain, a term which, as Wiktionary notes, 'In medieval texts, the term often refers to the northernmost part of the island, beyond the Forth and Clyde. Jean Markale, sometime Professor of Celtic Studies at the Sorbonne in Paris, suggested the name as having originally been applied specifically to the land of the Picts.

In Henderson's *Survivals in Belief among the Celts* he tells us the following;

I noted a children's game in Eriskay called *Mathair Mhor*, 'Big Mother', where the mother was feigned to be a pig! It is possibly a relic of early ritual.

1911, p.2

There is another strange remnant in the Halloween celebrations in Wales where, after hilltop celebrations including feasting, dancing and leaping through fires, the participants would run down the hill to escape the *hwch duu gwta*, the tailless Black Sow, who it was believed would take the last person on the hill, presumably to Annwn, the Underworld (Frazer, 1957 p.832).

Lewis Spence in his somewhat speculative *The Magic Arts in Celtic Britain* has the following:

> The pig or sow seems to have had an occult significance in bardic lore. The bardic initiates were frequently addressed or known as 'pigs'; ... The Gauls had a god known as Moccus, 'the Pig', and the animal was regarded as symbolic of the powers of fertility.
>
> 1995, p.160

A telling reference to the sow occurs in the 15th century poem referred to above about the creation of North Berwick Law. In it,

> The carling schup her in ane sow and is hir gaitis gane
> Gruntlying our the Greik sea...
>
> Watson 1995, p.141

Which means she changed herself into the shape of a sow and went off grunting over the Greek sea. This is quite explicit and though the poem is humorous and bawdy we clearly see the original goddess figure changing herself into a sow. The poem also states explicitly that all of this took place long before the Fall, the expulsion of Adam and Eve from the Garden of Eden, underlining the antiquity of the figure of the Carling or Carlin.

On the west of Scotland one of the stories associated with the Corryvreckan whirlpool – the third biggest in the world – has a sow swimming out from it and landing on nearby Craignish peninsula. Here it gave birth to nine piglets which scattered to become the ancestors of all the wild boar in Scotland. That this is potentially a remnant of something from the pre-Christian past may be deduced from a story about St Columba that was told in the area. He was handing out food to people in a time of famine when he was approached by a woman who had nine piglets in a chest back in her house. The saint realised this and refused to help her. When she disguised herself and came again to beg for food, he commanded her to go home. She did so and opened up the chest to find that her nine piglets had been changed to rats which jumped out of the chest and scattered to become the ancestors of all the rats in Scotland.

In both P- and Q-Celtic, and Scandinavian traditions we thus have strong evidence for the importance of porcine animals, male and female, and suggestions that the sow in particular was associated with goddess figures. The pig however had a wide provenance as such a symbol,

> The pig, a symbol of fertility in many cultures, was Demeter's favourite animal. A sow often appeared at her side. Artists portrayed Isis, the Egyptian goddess of fertility, giving birth n the back of a pig. In the wild, packs of roaming pigs are led by the eldest sow, making pigs one of the few animal societies that are organized as a matriarchy. A rotund animal that thrives in mud, grows quickly, and is very fertile can serve as an appropriate metaphor for pregnancy.
>
> Shlain 1998, p.111

The pig symbol also survives in Scottish folklore in various forms. In Orkney, which it has been suggested was named from the *Orci* or pig people (Wainwright 1955, p.135), the curious custom of killing a sow on 17 December, survived until the end of the 18th century. Because of this it was called Sow Day (Brown 1965, p.292).

Cattle

Cattle crop up on various Pictish symbol stones, sometimes alone and sometimes in conjunction with other animals and symbols. Probably the best known are the series of single bull stones from Burghead [FIG. 7]. These stones are difficult to fit in to the overall

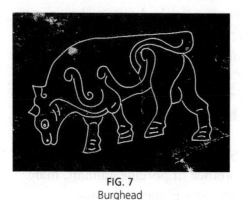

FIG. 7
Burghead

classification of the symbol stones but given that they appear without any other associated symbols, they are generally interpreted as being Class 1. Bulls are a widespread symbol of fertility and, in particular, virility, and the role of cattle in early British tribal society can hardly be over-estimated. Cattle raiding was of fundamental economic importance within tribal society and continued well into the clan period where cattle continued to be the primary object of moveable wealth – individuals and clans counted their wealth in numbers of cows. This importance actually outlasted the clan system and the importance of cattle in the later Highland economy has been explored in Haldane's *The Drove Roads of Scotland*. Before this, cattle were also the focus of one particular aspect of warrior activity in clan society, just as it had been in early Pictish times – cattle raiding. In fact throughout much of Eurasia such raiding was, for a considerable period, the normal behaviour for tribal warriors. As noted above, the centrality of the raiding or cateran tradition to the warrior clans of the Highlands a few centuries back (Alexander 1877, p.65) is a direct echo of Dio Cassius's reference to the natives in 2nd century Scotland as being 'addicted to raiding', and harks back to the Iron Age when such raiding was commonplace across Eurasia (Ginsburg 1991, p.236). As stated below (p.83), the stone from Dull in Perthshire [FIG. 8] appears to show a warrior band setting out on precisely such a raid, accompanied by dogs, no doubt trained to herd cows in total silence.

It was a regular activity amongst the warriors of the clans when each autumn the young men, and some older, more experienced ones, would head off over the hills to steal cattle from another clan. Cattle were the clear manifestation of moveable wealth and 'lifting' them gave a chance for the warrior to show his skill and, if caught in the act, show his courage and control of arms. The British government's portrayal of the post-Culloden Jacobites who resorted to this practice as nothing more than thieves, took no account of the fact that they were following what had been their traditional

FIG. 8
Dull

practices for centuries if not millennia. Burt goes into considerable detail of the traditional practices associated with this activity, explaining that to the Highlander the 'lifting' of cattle was not theft, but the action of a gentleman Highland warrior (1998, p.227ff). This has echoes in ancient story.

One of the best known of early Irish tales is the Cattle Raid of Cooley (*Tain Bo Cuailgne*) in which the warriors of the province of Connacht attack Ulster to capture the Brown Bull of Cooley for their queen, Maeve. (Rolleston, 1986 pp.203ff) She already had the White Bull of Finnbenach and in the end, after many heroic deeds involving the great hero Cuchulain, the bulls themselves fought on the Plain of Aei and the Brown Bull triumphed. This is one of the greatest of Early European epics and the centrality of the bulls to the story shows the importance of cattle. These bulls were said to have once been two swineherds from the land of the Sid (Shee), or fairies, who were reborn in animal form. This again suggests the possibility of ancient belief. A recent interpretation of stories associated with the mounds of the Sid, chambered cairns and tumuli, suggests that these, like the stories of warriors sleeping inside notable hills were in fact memories of rites carried out at communal graves. Such rituals would be focused on communicating with the ancestors, effectively asking them to work their influence on the newly sown seed crops to ensure they grew the following year. We will look again at tales associated with the burial mounds. There is also a probable link between these burial sites and the widespread folk tale motif of the musician or musicians who are lured into a Sidh, or fairy mound, to play for the fairies, reappearing to find that the one night they thought they had spent playing for their fairy hosts had in fact been a century or more.

In both Irish and Welsh stories we come across magical cows which come out from these fairy mounds or from lakes, and such tales also survived in Scotland. One instance of this is the white cow that was said to have come from Loch Roag to the great stone circle of Calanais on Lewis in a time of famine. This magical beast kept the community going by giving a pail of milk to anyone who approached her, till a local witch, to whom it had refused a double helping, milked it into an empty bucket at her next turn, after which the cow returned to the Loch.

Another tale, this time from Wales, tells of similar beasts. This is from HRE Davidson's *Roles of the Northern Goddess*,

> The fairy wife who came out of the lake in the popular tale from Llyn Y Fan Fach in Carmarthernshire in Wales, brought with her a wonderful herd of cows. When her husband broke the contract made at their marriage, she returned to the lake and summoned her cattle to follow her, calling various animals by name.
>
> 1998, p.66

There are a whole series of such Welsh tales, from different locations and often involving a white bull and black cows. The fairy wife mentioned above, long after her return is said to have sent out such a group of cattle to her newly-married grandson. After he and his wife died, the magic cattle returned to the lake. The connection with water and the supernatural female are strongly suggestive of ancient pagan belief.

The bull has often been interpreted as the masculine symbol par excellence. However, fertility itself was generally associated in pre-Christian times with the feminine aspect of nature – and it is one of the complex concepts of intertwined ideas in symbolism that the magnificently masculine bull can be regarded as a symbol of the goddess.

As late as the 17th century, bull sacrifice was known in Scotland. This is from Marian McNeill's *The Silver Bough*,

> It is recorded that in 1678 Hector Mackenzie, in Mellon of Gairloch, together with his son and grandson, sacrificed a bull on St Mourie's Isle (Isle Maree) in Loch Maree, 'for the recovery of Christina Mackenzie, who was formerly sick and valettudinarie': and again we read in the Records of the Presbytery of Dingwall that in 1695 the inhabitants were discovered to have been in the habit of sacrificing bulls on the feast day of the saint (August 15th), with 'other idolatrous customs,' including the circumambulations of the chapels associated with the saint's memory and the practice of divination rites.
>
> 1959, vol 1, p.59

The startling thing here is that the people at Dingwall were 'in the habit' of making such sacrifice, which was clearly something that had come from pre-Christian times. Did the local ministers before this know about the practice? If so, were they complicit in not drawing earlier attention to the practice? After all, this is more than a century after the Protestant Reformation had seen an attack on many 'idolatrous practices' which were associated in the minds of many with 'Romish practices'. It is ironic that such survival could continue in the Highlands where much of the population remained Catholic. Even today, Scotland has several fire-ceremonies, such as those at Biggar, Burghead, Comrie and Stonehaven, whose antiquity, in some cases, is beyond calculation.

Gimbutas, writing of a much earlier period, the 4th Millennium BCE and before, in the Balkans, tells of the importance of cattle symbols and particularly horns which she suggests were represented in the architecture of many goddess shrines.

There is a morphological relationship between the bull, on account of its fast growing horns, and the waxing aspect of the moon, which is further evidence of the bull's symbolic function as invigorator.

1982, p.91

Such extensive references to cattle in pre-Christian tradition probably first arose out of the centrality of cattle to the economic systems of tribal society and the importance of these beasts in sustaining life gave them an exalted position. Today in Africa, there are still cattle-herding societies where the cattle are treated with something close to reverence. Like much of ancient pagan thought, the importance of cattle as a symbol would appear to have been rooted in everyday reality.

The central economic role of cattle gave them a great importance in tribal society in the Highlands and they are central to some ritual behaviour. Beltane was one of the great feasts of the Old Year and time and again is the time chosen for the action to begin in traditional stories. The fires of Beltane which have long been the focus of interest in old ritual may well have arisen from the need to look after cattle. The Beltane 'shifting' of cattle to the shielings where they could feed on the grass of the high meadows came after their ritual purification between Beltane fires, practices which survived in to the 19th century as extensively noted by Banks (1937), Frazer (1978) and others. Though many commentators have noted the supposed 'Druidical' origin of the Beltane fires there is another aspect to them. The fires were made with different kinds of wood, one of which was juniper. It has long been known that juniper smoke has antiseptic properties and driving cattle between two fires giving off juniper smoke may well have been a means of killing off ticks and other vermin before the cattle were sent to grow fat in the hill pastures (Juniper URL).

Many of these instances of 'magical' cattle are linked to ideas of fertility but on one level their importance can be seen as rooted in everyday life, just as ideas relating to the Mother Goddess were associated with observed physical localities in the landscape that were reminiscent of her (see below).

Deer

Deer occur on all classes of the stones from the magnificent reindeer on the Class I Grantown-on-Spey Stone [FIG. 9] through to the ornate and complicated hunting scenes on the Class III Cross-slabs of Easter Ross. While the Grantown deer is the only surviving example of a complete deer on a Class I stone there are also deer heads on several stones. In that we know that Pictish sculptors were expert in their portrayal of animal life, these heads are clearly something other than severed heads of animals. The decoration on the bottom of these representations from Glamis Manse, Dunachton, and Meigle I stones [FIGS. 10, 11, 12] can be seen as suggesting that these are discrete objects in themselves, and are, I believe, masks, the added lines on the heads representing some form of tie. The animal heads on the Norrie's Law pins and possibly that on the missing Monifeith plate are similar and there is some resemblance, though in a rougher style, in the deer head from the Doo Cave at East Wemyss. On Rhynie 5 [FIG. 13] there is another symbol which has been interpreted as a dog or a seal but which I suggest as a possible deer costume, again outlined below. The deer head on the Ardross stone does not fit in with either of these but this is perhaps because it survives in an incomplete form. Referring to caps, an integral part of the shaman's costume, Eliade informs us, 'the commonest type is the one representing reindeer horns'. (1989, p.155).

It has often been suggested that the hunting scenes which occur on so many Class III stones are some sort of status symbol for the patrons of the stones, but we have no evidence to suggest that such patrons existed. What is clear is that many such stones are close to major Christian centres and may have been created by the monasteries or abbeys themselves. I see the tradition of the stones arising from a shared tribal consciousness of the world, through the ideas of a form of pagan religion, and there is no hard proof to suggest that even the later stones were specifically created for members of a putative tribal aristocracy. It is possible, however, that what we have in these scenes is a motif for the passing of paganism itself, the deer having such a complex and integral role in so much

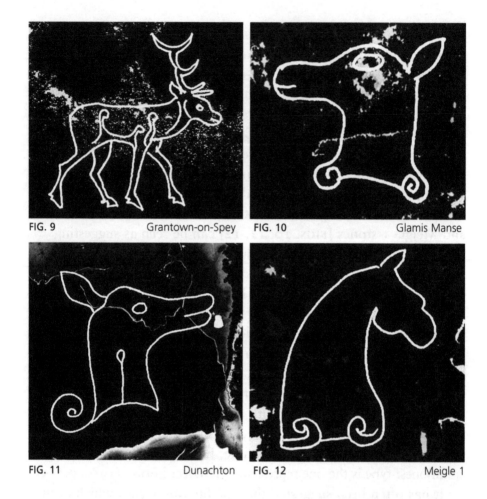

FIG. 9   Grantown-on-Spey   FIG. 10   Glamis Manse

FIG. 11   Dunachton   FIG. 12   Meigle 1

of what we know of the essentially pagan traditions of the early British peoples, among both the P- and Q-Celtic-speaking tribes.

In many northern European and Asian societies the deer is a powerful and recurrent symbol. Jacobson, talking of the Scytho–Siberian artistic tradition tells us,

> At the centre of that tradition, shared across the Eurasian steppe was the image of an antlered animal – sometimes a deer, at other times more closely resembling an elk... However its position may have varied within the Scytho–

Siberian symbolic system, the deer remained over time as the dominant image in the nomads' visual pantheon...

1993, p.22–3

In Scotland, the deer is often associated with the various figures of the Cailleach – the ancient dual Mother Goddess in her winter aspect. Time and again deer are referred to as the 'cattle' of the Cailleach (Mackenzie 1935, p.152) and there are many tales of hunters praying to her for success in the hunt before setting out after deer. There is some evidence to support the idea that there were cults of deer priestesses (Mackay 1934) and perhaps some of the folk customs that survive south of the border, such as the rituals at Abbot's Bromley and elsewhere, are an echo of this. Marija Gimbutas found strong associations of the deer and the goddess in Ancient Europe and links to the deer as a spirit animal, and possibly as a direct referent to the goddess herself, survived in shamanism well into the last century (Jacobson 1993, *passim*).

Within the Gaelic traditions of both Scotland and Ireland, there are many tales of the great hero Finn MacCoul. The story of Finn MacCoul's son Oisin (Ossian) which means 'fawn', is that he was born after Finn's wife Sadv was spirited away and turned into a deer by an evil druid. This is what Jean Markale says in his *Women of the Celts*,

Ultimately everything leads back to the story of Sadv (Grainne), the hind in the woods who was pursued so fiercely by the Black Man (Druid), the Druid who represented the social and religious order, but protected by Fionn and the Fianna, the last champions of Our Lady of the Night. For Finn's real name (Finn, 'handsome', 'white', or 'fair', being a nickname) was Demne, which suggests an ancient dam-nijo (small Deer); his son was Oisin, 'the Fawn'; and Oisin's son was called Oscar, which means he who loves the deer... Indeed the whole epic cycle of Finn, is placed under the symbolic patronage of the deer... All this is enough to make

Sadv (Grainne) and the story of Oisin particularly significant; for the hind goddess, or goddess of hinds is related to the most ancient image of Artemis – Diana, the sun goddess of these people who came to Western Europe before the Indo-Europeans.

1986, p.111

While there are problems with the very idea of Indo-European people, as defining people ethnically by the language they speak is inherently unsound, what Markale says is significant. He shows that within Gaelic tradition, like much of the rest of Europe, deer had a notable place. The changing of Sadv into a hind by the malevolent magician might be a reference to shape-shifting, an attribute of many goddess figures in Celtic mythology and also a common attribute of the priestesses of the Goddess and a group who seem to have succeeded them in some sense – the witches (McHardy 2002, Ch 8).

JG Mackay published an article on Deer Goddess cults in the Scottish Highlands in *Folklore* (1934, v 51). In this, he cites numerous examples of Highland tales which refer to the Cailleach associating with deer. Mackay presents the Cailleach as the Hag or Witch but following Mackenzie (1935, p.136ff.), I suggest she is in fact a remnant of belief in a Mother Goddess and she is often presented in these tales as being a giantess. Mackay tells us,

> The gigantic stature of these Old Women, their love for their deer, the fact that their dealings are almost exclusively with hunters and the fact that each is referred to as a bean-sidhe, or supernatural woman seems sufficient warrant for calling them Deer Goddesses.

1935, p.150

It was common for hunters who were after deer to pray to the Cailleach or Cailleach Bheur (biting) before setting out. Mackay thought that the Cailleach is an import from Ireland but there are good grounds for seeing her as an indigenous being, not least the number of mountains named after her and the numbers of mountains with which she is associated in story. That there are cultural links with Ireland is unarguable, after all we do know that people have been passing back and forth between Ireland and Scotland since the Stone Age – the similar megalithic traditions point to peoples who were very closely linked and the probability of trade, intermarriage and exchange of ideas both technological and spiritual is obvious. However, as there are so many tales concerning the Cailleach in Scotland, and she is matched in Scots oral tradition by the figure of the Carlin, it seems safe to assume that she is indigenous. The Cailleach is also known as the Cailleach Bheur (biting) in her association with the seasons, particulary winter – precisely matched by the Gyre Carlin figure – and was believed to have resided on Ben Nevis, the highest mountain not just in Scotland but the entire British Isles. She is the aspect of the Mother Goddess as Winter Hag and as McNeill tells us (1959, p.21) she was said to try to keep Bride, Goddess of Spring, imprisoned so that winter would remain on the land. We must remember that until just a few centuries ago, other than the young men going raiding, women and children in particular would not travel very far from their birth-places – possibly a few miles to summer shielings and into the next glen or so on very special occasions. Because of this the tales in which their beliefs were passed on were told within the compass of the audience's perceptions – the landscape within which they lived. This was particularly important in telling stories to children, which was how they were educated in the pre-literate world.

The deer plays as a constant theme in Gaelic legend and myth in particular – there are strong associations with fairies, deer sometimes being referred to as fairy cattle, and Mackay believed that tales of female figures associated with deer are sometimes references to priestesses of the goddess rather than the Goddess herself and says,

The deer priestesses never appear in the tales as priestesses, but as witches. They gave hunters blessings and charms to procure them success in the chase, and afterwards shared the spoils of the chase with them. After all witches are only fossil priestesses, the exponents of dead pagan faiths.

1934, p.168

Later he makes the following point,

Some deer priestesses, because probably they had wearied of paganism and the tedious yoke it laid upon its votaries, and perhaps because they loved some hunters, appear in tales as the Alternating Deer-Women, and marry their hunter lovers and live happily with then ever after.

Ibid., p.169

This is a reference to more shape-shifting and he goes on to suggest that stories of deer-transformations may well have been the deer-priestesses taking off and/or donning their costumes.

It is in this concept of the taking off of a deer costume that I think we can see something else in the Pictish Symbols. The strange shape that occurs on the Rhynie stone No. 5 [FIG. 13] which has been suggested as a dog or seal, can be seen as a representation of the priestess costume which Mackay refers to. In the Gaelic tale 'The Widow's Son', in JF Campbell's *Popular Tales of the West Highlands*, we have the following passage;

… he went out on three successive days. On the first, when he aimed, he saw over the sight a woman's face and breast, while the rest remained a deer. 'Don't fire at me, widow's son,' said the deer; and he did not, and went home and did not tell what had happened. The next day when he aimed, the woman was free to the waist, but the rest was still deer; and on the third she was free; and she told the hunter that she was the king of Lochlann's daughter, enchanted by the old man, and that she would marry the hunter if he came to such a hill.

1994, vol 2, p.62

Is this a portrayal of a deer-priestess actually taking off her costume? Many other societies throughout the world use animal costume and in European terms this habit can be traced back as far as the cave-painting at Trois Freres, though there the figure is patently male, although perhaps the male genitalia are part of the animal being used as a costume. The occurrence of the deer motif on early Pictish stones, I suggest, is directly linked to ideas considered in Mackay's paper on the Deer

FIG. 13
Rhynie 5

cult as one aspect of belief in the Goddess, and it is interesting to note the continuing significance of the deer as the quarry in the hunt scenes on later, Christianised Symbol Stones. As a further reflection of the potential importance of the deer in the distant past, a dowser in south-west England known as Donovan the Diviner suggested, on a television programme broadcast in 1989 (Donovan URL), that the earliest stone circles were built on the sites of deer-rutting stands. He says that in dowsing such stands and stone circles he discovered almost identical patterns. It makes sense that if the deer was seen as an aspect of the goddess the places where they mated would be full of particular fertility magic. Whether the deer are creating the lines or attracted by them is an interesting point but the significance of the association with fertility is self-explanatory.

Deer are not restricted to appearances in Q-Celtic traditions. Within Welsh tradition, much of which, I have argued, was originally shared with the P-Celtic-speaking Picts, there are also clear indications of the importance of the deer. In the story of St Kentigern's stay in Wales, he yoked a deer and a wolf together to pull a plough at the site of his church at Lampeter. This act of breaking ground to plant crops in new ground at a new location is of considerable significance in itself. Here we have the deer, a symbol of fertility in its many instances through its Goddess associations, and the wolf, usually a symbol of rapacity being linked together under the influence of an early Christian saint. It is likely that such tales were meant to have an influence on pagan and recently pagan peoples in the Dark Ages. Another figure from within the P-Celtic tradition is Merlin, who possibly arose initially from the Wild Man of the Woods, Lailoken, in the story of St Kentigern. In a Breton story mentioned by Markale (1986, pp.107–8), he arrives at the re-marriage of his wife Gwendolyn riding a stag and driving a herd of deer before him. As he approaches the happy couple, he tears off the stag's antlers, throwing them at Viviane's husband and killing him, before turning and riding back to the forest.

In the Mabinogion, the great collection of early Welsh traditional material, much of which would have been known and understood by the Picts, there are several instances of deer hunting. The later medieval royal deer hunts, may in some way have influenced how these stories developed but underlying them are ideas that are clearly much older. In the Mabinogion story of Geraint, son of Erbin, Mafawg son of Twrgadarn comes to Arthur's court and tells him of a magnificent white stag in the forest which they decide to hunt. Gwalchmei (Gawain) says to Arthur (p.190),

> ... were it not meet for thee to permit him whom it should come in his hunting to cut off its head and give it to the one he would wish, either to his own lady love or to his comrade's lady love.
>
> Jones & Jones 1989, p.190

This association with the deer and women also occurs in medieval Arthurian Romance, and Markale gives us this from Chretien de Troyes' 'Erec et Enide',

At Easter, King Arthur, who was holding court at Cardigan, announced that he wished to hunt the white deer 'in order to revive the custom'. Gawain, who was not in complete agreement, declared, 'We all know about the custom of the white deer. He who kills it must give a kiss to the most beautiful woman of your court.'

Ibid., p.107

It seems likely that this is based on a tradition where there would originally have been more than a kiss involved and in Gawain's reaction we are perhaps seeing a Christian's revulsion against what had been initially some sort of pagan fertility custom.

One further aspect of some of this material is the suggestion of shape-shifting. This has been interpreted as a reference to some sort of shamanic-type trance because of the existence of animal guides who help the shaman in his trance journeys. I have looked at many instances in ancient European tradition where priestesses are said to have been involved in shape-shifting and divination (McHardy 2003). If Mackay is correct in discerning traces of deer-priestesses in Gaelic tradition it seems certain that these are pre-Christian. Remembering that many Scottish Highland clans claim descent from Pictish ancestors and that most of the Highland area was within what is thought of as Pictland, it would hardly be surprising to see remnants of such beliefs and practices also occurring in the Symbol Stones.

As an example of the tenacity of traditional belief McKay tells us

A gamekeeper at Corrour Lodge, Inverness-shire, told my friend Mr Ronald Burn, in 1917, that the Cailleach of Ben Breck, Lochaber, had cleaned out a certain well, and had afterwards washed herself therein, in that same year. And in 1927 the late Dr Miller of Fort William, Lochaber, informed me that the old Cailleach is still well-known there.

1934, p.166

There are other examples of the importance of deer as a Symbol of the Goddess in Europe. This from Gimbutas's *The Goddesses and Gods of Ancient Europe,*

> The role of the deer in Old European myth was not a
> creation of Neolithic agriculturalists. The importance of a
> pregnant doe must have been inherited from a pre-agricultural
> period. The northern people in the hunting stage still believe
> in the mother of the universe as a doe-elk or wild reindeer
> doe. Myths speak of pregnant women who rule the world and
> who look like deer: covered with hair and with branching
> deer's horns on their heads. In the Upper Paleolithic era,
> similar images probably existed all over Europe.
>
> 1982, p.171

Deer carvings from an earlier period are found at Ballochmyle in Ayrshire (Ballochmyle URL), Glen Domhain, Kilmartin (Glen Domhain URL), Blackford Hill (Blackford Hill URL) and perhaps at Eggerness in Galloway (Eggerness URL), though Hicks sees the latter as circa 6th century (1993, p.51). At Ballochmyle the deer is part of an extensive panel of cup-and-ring carvings, while the Glen Domhain one is in an area spectacularly rich in such carvings. These suggest that the use of the deer symbol had been around for a very long time, underlining a potential continuity in belief over millennia. While two of the animal carvings at Eggerness are difficult to identify with any exactitude – they could be either horses or deer – another is clearly a deer, and along with the Ballochmyle and Glen Domhain carvings reinforce the idea that the carving of animal symbols in Scotland was not brought about by external influence after the Roman invasion of England.

Dog

The symbol often referred to as the wolf, on Ardross [FIG. 14] and two other stones lacks the notable peaked ears of a wolf and is therefore more likely to be a dog of some kind. Its general 'wolfishness' may well be due to it being, like all other domesticated canines,

FIG. 14
Ardross

originally descended from a tame wolf. The dog is often associated with hunting and perhaps the most famous of these is Bran, Finn MacCoul's legendary and magical hound, whose fearlessness was often stressed. The dog is seen as a symbol of both bravery and loyalty and many of them figure in the deer-hunts on later Pictish Symbol Stones. Probably the first animal to be domesticated, the dog has maintained an important role in human societies for millennia.

On one specific Symbol Stone, there are dogs which are totally dissimilar. This is the Dull stone from Perthshire and the dogs on it are small terrier-like animals. As there are no Christian symbols associated with this stone, it can be included as a Class I stone though the figures on it are carved in light relief rather than outline. I think this stone may well represent an actual raiding party setting out to 'lift' the cattle of a faraway tribe. It is noticeable that these dogs are also totally different from the deer-hounds included in the hunting scenes on so many later stones. These hunting scenes have been interpreted as in some way referring to putative patrons who paid for the creation of later stones – the idea being that such hunting on horseback is an essentially aristocratic pastime. As the idea of aristocracy within tribal systems is nonsensical perhaps these hunting scenes have another meaning. Given the role of the deer in so much indigenous folklore it would seem perfectly apt for the 'cattle of the Cailleach' as they were known, to be used in scenes, which perhaps are representing the triumph of Christianity over the earlier religion in a way that would be perfectly understood by contemporary society. After all, the usurpation of the symbol stones by the new religion seems unarguable and putting this sort of message onto a stone can be interpreted as a direct reminder of the new dominant spirituality.

Eagle

Eagles are associated with warriors as a symbol of bravery in many cultures and in Scotland the wearing of an eagle's feather was a sign of a chief or chieftain.

Logan 1831, p.276

The Eagle stone in Strathpeffer [FIG. 15] is unusual in that it is directly associated with a clan, the Clan Munro. One local tradition suggests that its original location marked the scene of a battle between the Munros and the Mackenzies while an alternative tale has it that the stone marks where a great eagle landed in its death throes after being thrown by the local chief from its eyrie high up on the hill of Knockfarrel where it had taken a child (McHardy 2005, p.121f.). This is an apparent case of clan totemism and the link with the story is underlined by the fact that the Crest of Clan Munro contains an eagle. A further local story associates the stone with the legendary Finn MacCoul and his Fianna, who play such an important part in the ancient story traditions of the Gaelic-speaking world in both Scotland and Ireland. The Tales of the Fianna are generally understood to come from pre-literate times and may well be as old as the Iron Age, if not older. These various stories echo the layering of cultural meanings that can be associated with symbols from a pre-literate society. Known locally as *Clach an Tiompain*, the stone of the drum, this stone may well have had some kind of ritual activity associated with it.

The idea of the eagle as a clan totem perhaps has some support from the Orkneys. One of the Symbol Stones with an eagle comes from the Broch of Birsay [FIG. 16] on the mainland of Orkney and it is worth considering if there may be a link here to the chambered cairn at Isbister on South Ronaldsay. The archeologist John Hedges commenting on the considerable number of sea eagle bones found in the cairn suggested that the people who created this structure may well have revered the sea eagle as some kind of tribal totem (Hedges 1984). The Broch of Birsay stone is unusual in that it has a

FIG. 15
Strathpeffer

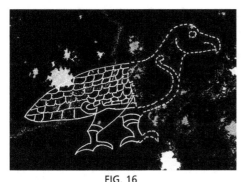

FIG. 16
Broch of Birsay Eagle

group of three armed male figures, the lead one having a more ornate hairstyle and dress than his companions. It is tempting to see some reflection of the ostentation of later clan chiefs in this.

Yet another eagle stone comes from Burrian, like Birsay, on mainland Orkney, and given the dating of the Tomb of the Eagles at Isbister is around 3000BCE this suggests a long-scale continuity of, at the least, the importance of the concept behind the symbol, whether or not specific ideas associated with it had changed.

Eagles turn up in a variety of Early Welsh stories. In the Mabinogion story of Math son of Mathonwy, (Jones & Jones 1993, p.47ff.) Llew Law Gyffes is turned into an eagle by the actions of Blodeuwedd who had tricked him into telling her the only way he could be killed. After this he flies off in the shape of an eagle to die. However, he is rescued and cured by Gwydion map Don, who then turns Blodeuwedd into an owl. This Mabinogion tale is full of magic and hints at what are likely to be traces of long lost beliefs.

Another Eagle turns up in an Early Welsh source. It is in the poem '*The Dialogue of Arthur and Eliwlod*' in which Arthur consults his nephew Eliwlod who has taken the shape of an eagle. Like Llew Law Gyffes in eagle form, Eliwlod is depicted as being perched in an oak tree, which may link these eagles to some form of ritual activity. Lewis Spence, who drew attention to the number

of mystical birds and animals that crop up in what he sees as the
'cultus' of Arthur that underlies the corpus of Arthurian tales, states;

> We may be justified in regarding this eagle-shape as
> indicative of psychic existence between life and death.
>
> Spence 1995, p.159

Whether or not this is true, we do seem to be dealing with some level
of remnant of an earlier belief system, involving shape-shifting. A
further reference to eagles turns up in the *Historia Brittonum,* by
the 9th century Welsh monk Nennius, where he tells us that 60
eagles live on 60 rocks in Loch Leven. It seems clear that he is
referring to Loch Lomond in which one of the islands is called
Inchcailloch. Inchcailloch has a *Tom na Nighean* or Mound of the
Maidens, conforming to a recurring duality we shall look at below.
Some commentators see these eagles as referring to separate tribal
chiefs, but as Nennius tells us of 60 islands and 60 rivers apart
from the 60 rocks, there seems to be a hint of something more
mystical here. The reference to Loch Leven (sic) is the first entry of
the section called the 'Wonders of Britain'.

Eliade tells us that the eagle as a symbol is widely used in both
costume and dance amongst the shamans of northern Eurasia
(1989, p.156ff), noting that this applies to both male and female
practitioners. Given that spirit-flight is such an intrinsic part of
shamanic tradition it may be that the shape-changing we find in
stories from among the Celtic-speaking peoples is connected to this
in some way. It suggests that we cannot rule out the possibility of a
similar meaning being related to the Pictish animal symbols
themselves. Beliefs among the tribal peoples of northern Eurasia
who have not gone through the hierarchic, centralising and
materialistic developments of 'Western civilisation' may well be
holding onto aspects of ancient belief and ritual that were once
much more common than they are now. The idea of Eurasian
Hunter Art, which emphasises underlying similarities of symbol and
potentially belief, may be reflective of a commonality or strong

similarity of such belief from the far past. Elsewhere I have noted that some of the beliefs associated with modern shamanism appear to reflect ideas that were widespread at an earlier date (McHardy 2003, p.151ff). Eliade goes on to say,

> The eagle is at the center of a mythical complex that includes the World Tree and the shaman's ecstatic journey. Nor must we forget that the eagle in a manner represents the Supreme Being, even if in a strongly solarized form.
>
> Ibid., p.158

In Norse mythology, Odin, after stealing the mead of poetry from the giant Suttung, changed into an eagle to escape, which, as Turville-Petre points out (1964, p.186), is very like the story of the Indian God Indra escaping in the form of an eagle when he had stolen *soma*, a hallucinogenic drink, from the god Tvashtri. Here we have the eagle associated in widely divergent cultures and suggestive of a very ancient origin for this idea. Both the mead of poetry and soma can be seen as not just inspirational, but ritual drinks. In this respect there are similarities to the Eurasian shamanistic practice of taking hallucinogens in the form of the fungus Amanita Muscaria, which some scholars have suggested was the original source for *soma*.

In his theft of the mead of poetry, Odin also changed into the form of a serpent (Turville-Petre 1964, p.36) which suggests tantalising possibilities for the combined symbols of eagle and serpent on the St Vigeans No. 2 stone, which is Class II [FIG. 17].

FIG. 17
St Vigean's 2

The various associations of the eagle; with bravery, as a putative clan totem, in shamanic trance, and in the ancient burial practice involving sea-eagles all suggest that the eagle symbol is a complex one that, while not directly involved with any obvious aspect of femininity, does appear to have a long provenance.

Goose

There is only one surviving example of a goose, on the stone from Easterton of Roseisle [FIG. 18]. It is obviously a goose, but whether a wild or domesticated bird is impossible to determine. As has been mentioned, Gimbutas and others have drawn attention to bird-goddess forms, but the symbolic uses of geese are relatively unknown. There is one source from Scotland. This concerns Mayo, one of the nine daughters of a putative early saint Donald who lived in Glen Ogilvy in the Sidlaw Hills north of the Tay. In the story, Mayo, the eldest of the nine, is said to have gone to speak to a flock of geese that were eating the corn seeds that her father had planted (McHardy 2003, p.21). This originally comes from Boece's 16th century *The History and Chronicles of Scotland* and while fragmentary it does have some of the connotations of power over animals and birds which has been attested to in various goddess forms. Gimbutas makes the point,

> Water birds, such as the crane, heron, wild goose, wild duck
> or grebe were sacred to the northern hunting tribes. Together
> with the bear and the elk they were venerated throughout
> the prehistory of northern Eurasia and in myth have not lost
> their importance to this day.
>
> 1996, p.134

She sees this process as arising from the importance of these birds and animals as a food source, reminding us that much of what we perceive of as myth and religion is rooted in everyday activity, and necessity. In France in particular, Mother Goose was a nursery rhyme character whose origin may be very old indeed. In the light of the following, it is also interesting that Ross (1993, p.300) mentions a depiction of the goddess Epona riding a 'great bridle-bearing horned goose'.

FIG. 18
Easterton of Roseisle

Horse

There is only one Class I Pictish symbol Stone which has a single horse on it in the manner of the other Class I animal symbols. This is at Inverurie [FIG. 19] in the shadow of the Bass, a massive man-shaped earthen mound, the name and shape of which is echoed elsewhere in Scotland (see below p.139). Horses were of considerable significance in early warrior societies and in the Mabinogion story 'The Dream of Rhonabwy' (Jones & Jones 1994, pp.119, 125) one of the warriors goes by the name of March, son of Meirchion. This translates as 'Horse, son of Horses' and he is perhaps better known as King Mark of Cornwall, in the Welsh tale of Tristan and Isolde. The Inverurie horse has been linked with the widespread Gaulish goddess figure Epona, (Anwyl 1906, p.41) and some have suggested a particular link with the Epidii, the tribe shown on Ptolemy's 2nd century map as living in the Kintyre peninsula. In a story about the Jacobite Rising of 1715, men from Kintyre are specifically said to have brought a large herd of horses to the Hanoverian garrison at Inverary, and the meaning given for the local surname MacEacharn is 'son of the Horseman'. Here, I would suggest, we have clear evidence of potentially remarkable cultural continuity over 1,500 years. Such an intriguing survival into modern times in a predominantly Christian country suggests that earlier continuities up to and beyond Pictish times might also have been tenacious.

In *Pagan Celtic Britain,* Anne Ross notes that the Welsh goddess Rhiannon is similar to Epona (1992, p.288). In the Mabinogion tales she appears variously as a magic horse herself, has to carry

visitors to the court on her back as if she were a horse and is made
to wear an ass's collar around her neck. She goes on to say,

> The evidence for the cult of a goddess especially concerned
> with horses in the insular tradition is strong, and... it may
> not be too far from the truth to suggest that the goddesses in
> whom fertility and maternity played a predominant part
> were connected with horses, but not of course, exclusively.
>
> Ibid., p.288

FIG. 19
Inverurie

And we must always
remember that the Picts not
only spoke a similar language
to the people of Wales but
that much of what has
survived in Early Welsh
sources originally derived
from Scotland. In this light, it
is worth mentioning the
theory put forward by
Oxenham. In his stimulating
*Welsh Origins of Scottish
Place-names* (2005, p.289ff.)
he suggests that the great Cross-slab of Hilton of Cadboll can be
interpreted in light of a Mabinogion tale. On the reverse side from
the cross, he suggests that what is depicted is a horse-mounted
Rhiannon in a scene from the Mabinogion tale of *Pwyll, Prince of
Dyfed*. If this is so, and it is not beyond the bounds of possibility, it
would suggest that the Mabinogi were not only known amongst the
Picts, but, as in Wales, the stories continued to be told long after
the institution of Christianity. In the light of the suggestions herein
it may be that there is more to be found in the Mabinogion, and
other early texts, both P-Celtic and Q-Celtic. The masculine bias of
most historical analysis to date, has led to layers of assumption
about early texts which may well obscure more than they clarify.

One way of counteracting this might be to consider how such tales may have been perceived by their original audiences, who may well have not been influenced by the unfortunate attitudes of early Christian writers towards the feminine in general, and women in particular.

Animal symbolism played a strong part in Norse traditions and Turville-Petre tells us,

> The beast most commonly venerated was the horse, or
> stallion, whose flesh provided the dish at sacrificial banquets.
>
> 1964, p.249

This suggests the horse had a strong role in both ritual and belief, but there are other horse links in Scandinavia. In Norse traditions there was a group of spirits called *disir*, who were generally held to be dead women, or perhaps ancestresses. Sometimes they take on the aspect of goddesses and Turville-Petre tells of a specific instance quoting from a poem called the Ynglinga Tal in which two *disir*, Ulf and Nari are identified with a horse goddess. He goes on to say,

> Freyja is the supreme *dis*: she is goddess of fertility and sister
> of the chief fertility god, Freyr. The horse is symbol of Freyr
> and his fertility and, at the same time, the symbol of death.
> And this explains why Hel (goddess of death) is the 'goddess
> of the horse'.
>
> 1964, p.226

There are those who believe that the Norse pantheon of Gods has been overly influenced by the Christian monks who first wrote about them, moulding them to the male dominated Greek pantheon with which they were familiar, and thus diminishing the importance of the goddesses.

The horse as symbol, as opposed to its later use in hunting scenes, can be seen as having strong associations with the feminine principle, through the figure of Epona and the Norse traditions.

Davidson points out that horses were used extensively in sacrifice in pre-Christian Scandinavia (1988, p.53ff).

Salmon

The salmon is another symbol that appears on the Pictish Symbol Stones and in early Irish and Welsh tradition [FIG. 20]. In Irish tradition there is the story of Connla's Well where the Salmon of Knowledge swims. It feeds on the magic nuts falling into the well from nine hazel trees surrounding it and thus attains great knowledge. This striking motif has been interpreted in many ways – one being that the five streams that flow from the well are representative of the five human senses. This well was considered in some Irish traditions to be the source of the River Boyne, and elsewhere is actually said to be under the waves of the sea, clearly marking it as an otherworld location. There were many wells in the landscape that were considered holy and the linking of this with the idea of sacred trees and the Salmon of Knowledge form a deep and entrancing pool of symbolism all on their own. I have been assured by a local that to this day there are wells in Argyllshire that have nine hazel trees planted around them. In Irish tradition it was from this well that the seven rivers of Ireland all originated. Rees and Rees say,

> ... and it has its counterpart in the Land of Promise where the five rivers that flow from it are the five senses.
>
> Rees & Rees 1961, p.161

Finn MacCoul gained his insight from an instance when he was learning with the Druid Finegas. The Druid had been trying for a long time to catch Fintan, the Salmon of Knowledge, but was only successful after Finn came to be his pupil. This is how Rolleston tells the story:

> Then one day he caught it, and gave it to Finn to cook, bidding him to eat none of it himself, but to tell him when it was ready. When the lad brought the salmon, Finegas saw

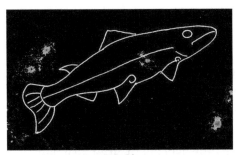

FIG. 20
Kintore

that his countenance had changed. 'Hast thou eaten of the salmon?', he asked. 'Nay,' said Finn, 'but when I turned it on the spit my thumb was burnt, and I put it to my mouth.' 'Take the Salmon of Knowledge and eat it, then' said Finegas, 'for in thee the prophecy has come true. And go hence, for I can teach you no more.'

1986, p.256

This is very like the story in Welsh tradition of Gwion Bach, who became the great bard Taliesin by a similar process, as we shall see. By sucking his thumb, Finn had assimilated the knowledge the Druid was hoping to acquire and subsequently if he needed to understand any problem all he had to do was suck his thumb. Given that he was a pupil of a Druid at the time this is clearly a reference to some level of sacred initiation, and the salmon is central to this idea.

It is striking that the importance of the salmon in pagan ideas seems matched by the importance of the fish symbol within early Christian traditions – one of many similarities that scholars have noted.

In the Early Welsh tale of Culwch and Olwen (Jones and Jones, 1994), Gwrhyr, Interpreter of Tongues is sent out by King Arthur to try and locate the whereabouts of Mabon son of Modron who was stolen from his mother when he was three days old. He seeks out the oldest of creatures and starts with the Ouzel of Cilgwri who in turn sends him to the Stag of Rhedynfre, who directs him to the Owl of Cwm Cawlwyd, who is older than him. The Owl then sends Gwrhyr to the Eagle of Gwernabwy who takes him to the even older Salmon of Llyn Llyw, who finally tells him that Mabon son of Modron is imprisoned far away but takes him there on his back and Mabon is rescued. These creatures, several of whom occur on Symbol Stones, are presented in terms of their increasing age, suggesting some idea of a continuity with the far past. Mabon himself is often interpreted as a god and son of Modron, a powerful female who corresponds closely to the idea of a Mother Goddess and has been seen as the equivalent of Matrona, the goddess of the river Marne in ancient Gaul.

Water is itself prominent in various aspects of pre-Christian belief and, as it is necessary for all life, it might not be a stretch to see it as being conceived of as the blood of the Goddess herself. The widespread reports of pagan rituals at wells in Scotland underlines this possibility and it is noticeable that the Cloutie Well on the Black Isle, which apparently has always been considered a healing well locally, has actually become a growing centre of pilgrimage over the past few decades, evidenced by the expanding offerings in the adjoining trees.

The salmon appears in itself to be a symbol of knowledge or insight and is also associated with the past. In tribal societies such as those of 1st Millennium Scotland, we can be relatively certain of the importance of the ancestors – echoed in the ongoing stature of the Seannachie in late clan society whose role on important occasions was to remember and recite the genealogy of the clan chief, and thus the clan itself – and the idea of the salmon as the oldest living being in the tale of Culwch and Olwen, suggests the possibility of a long continuity of the symbolic role of the salmon.

While there seem no clear grounds for interpreting the salmon as linked directly to the idea of the feminine, the idea of the salmon in the well links to the numerous instances of wells having direct relationship to both spirituality and healing, often in association with female figures.

Serpent

In many cultures and at many times, the serpent has been seen as symbolic of wisdom, often of a malevolent character. In the ancient idea of Ourobouros (origin), the serpent eating its own tail, people have seen a reference to the turn of the seasons, the whirling of the stars through the precession of the equinoxes over 26,000 years and even life itself. In the Christian belief system the serpent is of course the cause of the downfall of humanity from its paradise life in the Garden of Eden. However there seems to be a precise meaning we can associate with the Pictish serpent. We know that what we see on the Pictish stones [FIG. 1] is an adder, the only true snake known in Scotland. In *The Silver Bough*, McNeill quotes a Lewisman talking of *a Clach Nathraich*, the Adder Stone, or 'Druidical Bead';

> A number of serpents (adders) congregating at certain times form themselves into a knot and move round and round on the stone till it is worn through, they pass and re-pass after each other through the hole, which by-and-by becomes hard. It is this slime which gives the stone the healing properties it is supposed to possess.
>
> 1957 p.91

Here we have a direct link between the adder and the Druids, considered by many to have been priests of the pre-Christian pagan religion in the British Isles. However, we have another link with the adder which is perhaps more telling. This is the association with the figure of Bride, in Hebridean Christian tradition the birthmaid of Christ, and undoubtedly descended from an earlier goddess figure who may well have been, as in Ireland, the patroness of poetry and fertility (Ross 1992, p.289f). I have suggested elsewhere (McHardy 2003, Ch 2) that Bride in Scotland is not descended from the Irish Brigid, as Ireland has never had snakes. As with the Cailleach we are perhaps closer to understanding how things were if we see the Bride being a part of common cultural inheritance between Ireland and mainland Britain rather than seeking to discern the specific influence of one specific culture, or language, over another. Although Bride is specifically associated with Imbolc (1st February), Beltane (1st May) is the start of summer, the season

FIG. 1
Newton Garioch

of Bride, and this is of course the time when, given that the sun is shining, adders can be seen sunning themselves on rocks in many parts of Scotland. Again, we have a practical reality involved in religious concepts.

In many societies, snakes in general are seen as representative both of the chthonic regenerative power of the earth and specifically of regeneration and rebirth. This is because snakes live on and in the ground, emerge in spring and slough their skins, which looks like a physical rebirth. Bride was Christianised as St Bridget whose perpetual holy fire at Kildare (the cell of the oak-tree) was tended, like Cerridwen's cauldron and its attendant fire, by nine holy women. An old Gaelic poem translates,

> 'Today is the day of Bride, the serpent shall come from the hole / I will not molest the serpent / Nor will the serpent molest me. Another version runs: 'The Feast Day of Bride / The Daughter of Ivor shall come from the knoll / I will not touch the daughter of Ivor / Nor will she harm me.'
>
> McNeill 1959, 2, p.27

Both these charms or incantations were originally reported in Carmichael's *Carmina Gadelica* and he explained that the daughter of Ivor was a reference to the adder, because a man called Ivor had sacrificed to the adder in the past. The Day of Bride was Imbolc, one of the quarter day feasts of the Celtic-speaking peoples, corresponding to the 1st day of February and the beginning of the period in which lambs were born. Bride is of course the Goddess of Spring and Summer and her battle with Beira, the Cailleach Bheur is probably one of the oldest myths we have.

The Day of Bride itself was associated with a great many propitiatory rituals including the creating and decorating of Bride's Bed with a representation of the goddess and a white wand, the '*slachdan Bride*' or rod of Bride, in the cot. There were ceremonies involving parades from house to house and the swastika shaped cross know as St Bridgit's Cross in Ireland was commonly hung up at this time of the year. Under the influence of Christianity, Bride became St Bridgit and there are dozens of references in Gaelic poetry, hymns and incantations to Bride as the birthmaid or foster mother of Christ eg 'I send witness to Mary / Mother who aids men / I send witness to Brigit / Pure tender Nurse of the Lamb'. The *Carmina Gadelica*, that wonderful collection of Gaelic hymns and incantations, has dozens of similar examples showing that even in her Christianised form, Bride continued to hold a place in the hearts of the Gaels. Bride is also closely associated with Beltane as we shall see.

FIG. 21
Cernunnos [Creative Commons]

FIG. 21a
Meigle 22

As Robert Graves pointed out in his *White Goddess,* the association of the serpent with the Mother Goddess is common throughout Europe and beyond. The symbol of the serpent is also common in Norse mythology and Hilda Ellis Davidson in *Lost Beliefs of Northern Europe* (1993, p.30) draws attention to the Cernunnos figure on the Gundestrup cauldron who is holding a serpent in one hand and has stag's antlers on his head [FIG. 21]. The similarity between this Cernunnos figure and the creature sometimes referred to as the Merman of Meigle on Meigle No. 22 [FIG. 21a] has been mentioned extensively. The adder symbol may be read as referring, at one level at least, to the figure of Bride. As we shall see, the figure of Bride herself appears to have been of fundamental importance in Scottish pre-Christian belief and it is noteworthy that Jhone Leslie in his 16th century *Historie of Scotland* claimed that Bride was indigenous to Scotland (1888, p.229).

Serpent and Z-rod

With the serpent, or adder, so strongly associated with chthonic powers it is tempting to see the serpent and Z-rod [FIG. 1] as in some way reflecting the duality of earth and sky (see Z-rod below p.117). While we can never be certain as to what people thought in the past, the idea of Sky Father and Earth Mother, does have a wide provenance. (Sky Father URL).

The 'Beastie'

This enigmatic symbol, over a dozen of which crop up on Class 1 stones, was long known as the Swimming Elephant [FIGS. 22, 23]. This name neatly describes the problems regarding this symbol. We do not know what it is supposed to represent. All the other Class 1 animal symbols are immediately recognisable – they are quite specific. The Beastie, on the other hand, appears to be a composite figure of some kind. It has some of the aspects of a marine mammal, and various theories have been advanced to suggest it may be a reference to an extinct creature, perhaps even a freshwater dolphin. Sadly, we have no evidence to support the idea that Scotland ever had such a creature. However, the real problem with this type of explanation is that the beast does not look like it ever existed. While the head and possibly the appendage to it certainly have echoes both of dolphins and even the blowhole of cetaceans, it is portrayed with legs. We can assume that the Picts knew what a dolphin, or similar creature looked like out of the water, either through seeing dead ones washed ashore, or perhaps by hunting them, yet this creature is not a dolphin. Like most Pictish symbols it crops up in a variety of forms – there is no one standardised representation of the symbol that everyone followed. This is in itself significant as it suggests that whatever the precise socio-religious structure that underpinned the creation of the Class I symbols, it was essentially localised. This is what one might expect, if, as I have suggested in *A New History of the Picts* (2010), the Picts were essentially tribal and

had been for a very long time indeed. As we shall see later, there is evidence in Scotland for a form of underlying spiritual belief pattern that seems to be localised. Because the Beastie it is the only one of the animal forms that is not recognisable, its form must have some kind of significance that perhaps

FIG. 22
Meigle 5

FIG. 23
Detail – The 'Beastie'

does not apply to the others. That it was a significant symbol can be taken as read from the number of Class I instances, but also the fact that it continued to be used on the later Class II stones which were created in the Christian period. In this respect, it may be that this is a specific example of the approach suggested by Pope Gregory to Bishop Mellitus in 609 (Bede 1955, p. 127). It is unlikely that we can ever be sure of precisely what it signified, though if we can come up with an interpretation of all, or most of the symbols, perhaps we can have more hope of understanding it. Hopefully the approach taken in this work may be of some assistance in this regard.

There is one particularly significant aspect of the fact that the Beastie appears to be a composite of animal forms from both land and sea. The concept of duality is one which appears time and again in dealing with the symbols and this may be an instance of that. As a composite animal, it is tempting to compare it to the well-known figure of the 'Sorcerer' from the Cave of Trois Fréres, Ariege, France (Sorcerer URL). This cave painting shows a human clad in what appears to be a variety of animal skins and has been interpreted as shamanic. Though the Sorcerer dates from the Paleolithic period in Europe, we must remember that if the Picts were our indigenous people they were heirs to millennia of their own traditions before Christianity came. Given the many suggestions that the Sorcerer was some sort of shamanic figure, it is possible that there is a link between this figure and the idea of the deer as a sacred image, and the representation of deer masks/costume that were possibly used in ritual. This, however, is totally speculative though the various references to the Sorcerer as a Deer-man do remind us of how deer are symbolically represented in ritual practices over a wide area and long periods (Jacobson 1993, *passim*).

Geometric shapes

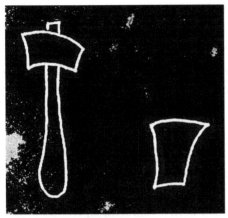

FIG. 24
Abernethy 1

FIG. 25
Kintore

FIG. 26
Congash

While the animal symbols, apart from the Beastie, are recognisable, some of the Class I symbols are not. The hammer and anvil from the Abernethy I stone [FIG. 24] are, I suggest, probably some sort of reference to the craft of the smith, but whether as an individual, a group or the personage of a god figure is unclear. Others are not so directly understandable and have given rise to various interpretations. I suggest that there is a potential link between some of them that conforms to the ideas so far presented. Some, like the floriated symbol on stones from Craigton, Pabbay and Dunnichen, the S-shaped figure from Kintore, [FIG. 25] Drimmies and East Wemyss and the peculiar 'bow and arrow' symbol from Congash [FIG. 26] seem impossible to make informed guesses about, but if there is merit to the suggestions given here, that may change in time. Others, like the in-filled rectangular shapes from a variety of locations, have been interpreted by some as comb cases but I am not convinced. The cauldron symbol is quite explicit but the double disc, with or without Z-rod is, like the crescent and V-rod open to a range of interpretations, all of which are essentially speculative. However, given the numbers of these last two, over 50 and 60 examples respectively, some attempt must be made at trying to decipher them. Others like the notched rectangle and Z-rod are also open to a variety of interpretations.

Cauldron

Representations of the cauldron obviously incorporate much of the symbolism of the circle (below p.104) but the cauldron has a specific set of associations. On Pictish symbol stones it can be seen as a large circle with two smaller circles – which has lead in the past to suggestions of the sun and two moons – with a double line running through the two smaller circles across the larger one [FIG. 27], and a side-on view as on the Glamis Manse Stone [FIG. 28]. These can

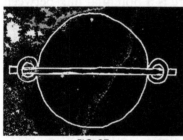

FIG. 27
Kintore

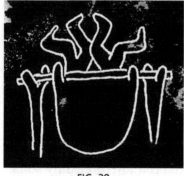

FIG. 28
Glamis Manse

all be understood as representing a clear picture of a penannular or ringed cauldron which we know was in common use throughout Dark Age Europe and had been for millennia. That such cauldrons were sometimes ritual objects is proved by the existence of the Gundestrup Cauldron, covered in 'Celtic' symbols and motifs and found last century in Denmark (Gundestrup URL). Cauldrons have also been found in votive hoards like that in Carlingwark Loch near Castle Douglas. 'Carlin' here is a reference to the Queen of the Witches figure, accredited with the creation of this loch, just as the Cailleach was credited with landscape changing in many places in Scotland.

In Welsh, Irish and Scottish traditions the cauldron has supernatural connotations. Cerridwen's cauldron occurs in the early Welsh poem *The Spoils of Annwn*, attributed to the semi-mythical bard Taliesin. Annwn was a sort of Underworld and Arthur and his companions went there to attack Caer Sidi, which can be translated as 'the Seat of the Fairies'. In the poem we have the following:

> By the breath of nine damsels it is warmed.
> Is it not the cauldron of the chief of Annwn in its fashion?
> With a ridge round its edge of pearls.
> It will not boil the food of a coward not sworn.
>
> Sacred Texts URL

Taliesin himself is closely associated with Cerridwen's cauldron. In an ancient tradition, the boy Gwion Bach is set to look after the cauldron of Cerridwen in which she is boiling up a magic potion to give her spectacularly ugly son Avaggdu the ability to understand everything. After a year, the three precious drops distilled from the process jump out of their own accord and land on Gwion's finger. He licks them off and immediately sees all. He knows that Cerridwen is aware of what is happening and in a remarkable scene he changes shape to try and escape her. First he becomes a hare and she chases him in the shape of a greyhound; he changes into a fish, she becomes an otter; and when he changes himself into a grain of wheat, she becomes a hen and swallows him. Nine months later, she gives birth to Gwion who is now Taliesin and unable to kill him, sets him adrift on a river in a basket, from which he is rescued by Gwyddno Garanhir and becomes in time a great bard. It is tempting to see some sort of reference in this shape-shifting to shamanistic practice, in that the shaman in his trance often experiences this process (Eliade 1989, *passim*).

The cauldron described in the Spoils of Annwn is interpreted as being the cauldron of poetry and inspiration and Cerridwen herself is clearly a goddess figure. Marian McNeill described this in *The Silver Bough*, we have the British Keridwen, Goddess of Nature who possesses a magic cauldron with three properties – inexhaustibility, inspiration and regeneration – symbolising the regenerative power of the earth.

1959, p.34

In the Mabinogion, the collection of early Welsh myth and legend, there are other cauldrons. In the tale of Branwen, Daughter of Llyr the mythological King Bendigeidfran is discussing reparations with Matholwch for an insult done to him by Branwen,

> 'I will enhance thy reparation still further,' said Bendigeidfran. 'I will give thee a cauldron, and the virtue of the cauldron is this: a man of thine slain today, cast him into the cauldron, and by tomorrow he will be as well as he was at the best, save that he will not have the power of speech.'
>
> Jones & Jones 1993, p.24

Another tale in the Mabinogion, Peredur Longspear, has the following,

> ... And at the beginning of their converse he could see a horse coming and a saddle on him and a corpse in the saddle, and one of the women rose up and took the corpse from the saddle, and bathed it in a tub that was below the door with warm water therein and applied precious ointment to it. And the man rose up alive, and came to where Peredur was and saluted him and made him welcome.
>
> Ibid., p.174

These are clearly vessels of rebirth and reincarnation and in a closely parallel Irish tradition we have the Cauldron of the Dagda, a truly ancient pre-Christian god figure, rather than a goddess. It could feed nine at a time, endlessly, but would not boil the food of a coward. In the tale of the Battle of Moytura it is said that warriors who were killed in battle could be restored to life if immersed in the cauldron of the Dagda, though when they came back to life they too had lost the power of speech. This perhaps means that they were forbidden to speak because they had crossed the threshold between life and death and then returned. This, I suggest, is what we see on the Glamis Manse Stone [FIG. 28] where two pairs of legs are seen protruding from a cauldron.

The importance of the cauldron may, I believe, be seen in Shakespeare's *MacBeth*. The famous witches' scene, where three wizened hags are boiling up a disgusting brew in their cauldron when MacBeth arrives to ask them to tell the future, might have a factual basis. Shakespeare was probably reacting to the fascination of King James I of England, and VI of Scotland, with witchcraft and demonology. However Otta Swire tells us of a tradition from Aviemore that says the Pictish kings used to come to consult three wise women on the future at Loch nan Carraigean, just to the north of the town on Granish Moor (1963, p.121). Other cauldrons turn up in Scottish witch tales and it is of particular interest that, as noted above, amongst the votive offerings recovered from Carlingwark Loch near Dumfries, there was at least one massive iron cauldron.

The remarkable Gundestrup Cauldron [FIG. 21], found in Denmark but thought to be of 'Celtic' origin and covered with motifs that seem to refer to mythological tales, was made of silver and is a remarkable sacred object illustrating the ritual importance of the idea of the cauldron.

One of the aspects of symbolism in pre-literate society is the fact that many of the symbols, while having many layers of symbolism attached to them, could at the same time be everyday objects. The cauldron was the primary source of food for the family and was cooked over a fire that was in the centre of the dwelling below a smoke hole. This would mean that people would sit in a circle, an act that has its own magical attributes, around the cauldron to eat. So in everyday life the cauldron was literally at the heart of every-day family existence while being a symbol of the goddess who can be interpreted as symbolic of all life itself. The cauldron can thus be seen as a cornucopia, or fount of all things good, and a symbol of continuity within the community. From birth all members of the family would have the symbol of the cauldron on the fire at the very centre of their existence.

There is another aspect to the cauldron which appears to be of some significance. The term *coire* in Gaelic, or corrie in Scots is a reference to a bowl, or cauldron-shaped area of the landscape. And as we shall see, also to one particular part of the seascape of Scotland as well.

Circles

In ECMS the varieties of decorated circle are gathered together under the heading Circular Disc (1993, I, p.58). As can be seen in the Cauldron symbol [FIG. 27], a simple circle can be symbolic of many things and is central to much sacred imagery all over our planet. All too often earlier scholars – looking for evidence of 'Sun Gods' – interpreted circles as representing the sun, while others have insisted on a feminine, lunar interpretation. Symbols can be that simple but at the very same time be capable of expressing complex and even contradictory ideas. The circle can be seen as representing the turning of the earth and the rotation of the seasons upon the earth. In early societies, ruled by seasonal animal migrations or the necessities of the agricultural year, the turning of the seasons was of fundamental importance – it has been suggested that all religion arises from humans calling for the sun to return after winter – a supposition that ignores the experience of human life between the Tropics where seasonal variation is less dramatic. The notion of the circle as the Great Serpent eating its tail, which has survived through many societies since Mesopotamian times, reflects this belief but also directly links us to the serpent in the sky – the precession of the equinoxes. Nobody knows for how long human societies have been aware that the length of time between tonight's precise constellations of stars above your head appearing again is 24,600 years, but this is one of the great mysteries that have been around for a long, long time. The use of any design within a circle can be seen as sanctifying and blessing it, putting it into a sacred perspective that emphasises the continual turning of time.

Only slightly less significantly, the Circle can also be seen as representing not just the unity of life but particularly the four primary directions, East, South, West and North. This is what probably lies behind the widespread motif of the cross in the circle which comes from millennia before Christianity was even thought of. When the tribes gathered at the great chambered tombs of Western Europe at Halloween to commune with their dead, there was a practical purpose. It seems likely that they were interceding with those who had gone before, and been put into the ground, and were asking them to nurture and germinate the seeds that had been planted in that same earth to create the next year's food. This too is part of the annual turning of the seasons played out in all early human societies, and symbolically contained in the simple line of a circle.

Crescent and V-rod

This symbol has gained a high level of popularity in recent years inspiring a whole range of pewter and silver jewellery, and other artefacts. [FIG. 29]. The symbol occurs on over 30 of the Class I stones, more than any other, and survives into the later Class II stones. It is found on many Pictish symbol stones – but no two are the same. All the surviving examples are unique. The crescent can be linked to the lunar crescent and the moon has long been associated with the feminine principle. It is also true that horned structures and figurines were common in Ancient European ritual and there may be a link. The V-divides the crescent into three and this may well be a direct representation of the three visible phases of the moon. There is no doubt that people in 1st millennium Scotland lived much closer to nature than we do today and the phases of the moon are of significance in the folklore of many societies. Regarding this, Cummins makes an intriguing suggestion,

The crescent, representing the moon, is shown upside down, an

orientation which must exist but is never visible. It is divided
by the V-rod into the three phases of the visible moon,
waxing crescent, round moon and waning crescent.

2009, p.91

This suggests that the lunar link is explicit, and in many societies
the moon can be understood as a symbol of the Mother Goddess
herself. The Crescent and V-rod is thus also symbolic of time and it
is worth noting that the ends of the V-rod are always different and
in many cases look like open and closed flowers. This too can be
read as a direct referent to time, in this case to day and night, when
flowers are respectively open and closed. This might also potentially
be interpreted as a reference to the dualism we find in Scottish
tradition in Bride, Goddess of Summer and the Cailleach, Hag of
Winter who can be seen as essentially one figure.

The infill of the Crescent and V-rods varies enormously [FIGS.
30, 31] but many of the curves recall the representations on pottery
noted by Gimbutas and could be interpreted as representing the
curves of the full female figure. In ancient times there were
certainly periods in which it was the full-body of a mature woman
who had given birth that was worshipped. Gimbutas draws
attention (1996, p.93) to the recurrent use of horns in early
Mediterranean altars that she associates with the Goddess. It is
perhaps not coincidental that this shape, based on the use of
bullhorns as a symbol of power and fertility, can be seen if one
inverts the Pictish crescent. Just
because we perceive one
specific meaning does not mean
there are no others and the
clearer a picture we can develop
of the belief patterns of the far
past, the better we can perhaps
understand the potential for
multiple interpretations of the
symbols. Philosophies and

FIG. 29
Lindores

FIG. 30
Moy

FIG. 31
Logie Elphinstone

mythologies change and grow but the concept of admiration of the mother as a representation of the mother goddess is a strong one.

One interesting reading of this symbol was given to Robbie the Pict, by an old French woman of mystical leanings. She said the crescent represented the female principle and the V was a broken arrow representing the masculine force in a non-threatening way. I cannot say she was correct, but one sensible, sympathetic reading does not rule out others. However, the vulvic V combined with the crescent is strongly symbolic of the feminine principle.

It is also perhaps significant that unlike the Z-rod, which occurs in conjunction with three other symbols on Class I stones, the V-rod has only ever been found with the crescent. Is this then a case where the feminine aspects of separate components of the symbol are being used to reinforce each other, making this a specific sign of the mother goddess herself?

Double crescent

Several of the stones have what is clearly a double crescent [FIG. 32], one on top of the other, back to back. Marian McNeill tells us,

> On tombstones at Luss, Stobo, Paisley, and many other places
> in Scotland we find a curious device – two crescents set back
> to back, representing the last quarter of the old moon and

FIG. 32
Kintore

the first quarter of the new. This is an ancient Pictish symbol of immortality; the moon died and was re-born every month.

1959, pp.58–9

This is a very definitive statement but an interesting interpretation, emphasising the fact that we are dealing with a long-term philosophic under-pinning to the use of the symbols on the stones. The idea of immortality McNeill suggests may be linked to that aspect of many tribal societies that is often erroneously referred to as ancestor worship. The reverence for the ancestors and the prayers to them are a recurrent fact in many societies and do seem to be linked to ideas of regeneration and rebirth. In one sense, the tribe itself can be conceived of as immortal in that the importance of the genealo-gical past is matched by the commitment to the future descendants of the tribe. This can be seen in the very name used for tribes in Scotland, 'clan', which derives from the Gaelic *clann*, meaning children.

The moon's effect on female menstruation is much-discussed and in many cultures, menstruating women have been seen as dangerous and kept apart from male society. Such lunar references suggest further significant links between Pictish symbols and what we know of magical practice in different parts of the world.

Double-disc

This widespread sign has been suggested as representing the sun in two seasons. Mackenzie tells us (1935, p.137) that in traditional Gaelic culture the year was divided into two seasons – The Time of the Big Sun and the Time of the Little Sun, summer and winter respectively. Summer began with Beltane, the great feast of 1st May and winter with Samhain (Soween) our Halloween, ushering in winter on 1st November. This was the time to speak to the ancestor spirits and pray for their help in ensuring the planted seed would rise again come spring – or even that spring/summer would come again. This symbol sometimes occurs with a Z-rod, which on this reading might underline its function as a strong sky symbol. As we know, there is always the possibility of several layers of meaning and perhaps the double disc also referred to the breasts of the goddess – the number of surviving Scottish place-names in Gaelic and Scots drawing attention to breast or nipple shaped hills and configurations is truly remarkable and includes Bennachie – *Beinn a Ciochan* (the Hill of the Paps), Meikle Pap and Little Pap on Lochnagar, the Paps of Jura and several instances of Maiden Pap from Caithness to the Borders. These will be considered in more detail below.

A sidereal interpretation of the double-disc does not of course rule out other such meanings. While we can never be sure of the primary meaning it is possible to suggest a series of interpretations that all link to aspects of Mother Goddess. The linked double disc might then be a referent to the year, much as I have suggested the open and closed terminal ends on V-rods can be interpreted as referring to day and night. Particularly in pre-industrial societies, people tend to be inherently practical and though there may be many layers of meaning in any one shape or group of shapes we should not overlook the obvious. If this is the case then it may perhaps have some links to the story mentioned by McNeill in *The Silver Bough*, where the Cailleach, Hag of Winter, drinks from a sacred well before dawn on Beltane and enters the new season as Bride, golden Goddess of Summer (1959, p.21).

An interesting interpretation of the double-disc with the Z-rod was made by Cummins (2009, p.75). He interprets it as referring directly to Drust, one of the Pictish Kings from the King lists. He makes the intriguing point that this symbol occurs at Trusty's Hill near the Solway Firth and sees this as a marker of a southern Pictish incursion. As I do not accept any of the arguments so far propounded for either the symbols or the symbol stones being personal memorials, and I believe that the idea of a 'king' before the coming of Christianity is anachronistic within tribal society, I find this a bit of a stretch. As I have stressed already, symbols in a pre-literate world can suggest more than one meaning and as Cummins suggests this association as occurring in the 5th century, it is not beyond possibility that a specific symbol became associated with an individual in a time when the old certainties of understanding the world had undergone significant change. However, as I suggest the symbols are part of a continuum of belief going back perhaps thousands of years, the idea that a symbol could be created for an individual would make no sense. Also, as stated in *A New History of the Picts*, (2010, p.37f.) Dio Cassius locates the Maetae, who he saw as one of the two main groupings of the Picts, in the lands directly to the north of Hadrian's Wall, so the idea of a raid from the north being commemorated in this way seems unlikely.

The double-disc is also a symbol that can be related directly back to earlier stone carvings where there are many instances of cup-and-ring markings occurring in pairs.

Mirror and Comb/Mirror and Comb Case

These symbols are in the main found together [FIG. 33] and many people have interpreted them as being a specific sign of femininity. While I see little grounds for considering these stones as markers of individuals, this certainly does not rule out familial or tribal references. Some of the symbols may well have had a role as totems within the different clans and some of the Class III stones may well have had patrons from the period when the tribes were forming proto-kingdoms. However, the problem with the idea of the mirror and comb, or comb-case, as a general sign of femininity, is that it is anachronistic. There are many references to the tribal warriors of Northern Europe, from Roman times on, as being concerned with their appearance. If they were tattooed how else would they see themselves unless with mirrors? We are also told in many sources that tribal warriors in northern Europe were vain about their hair and moustaches. The idea that only women have vanity is frankly ridiculous and probably arises from Victorian ideas of women's role in making themselves presentable, for men. Samson (1992, p.58) notes that there are no strong archaeological or cultural grounds for assuming that combs and mirrors must be associated with females.

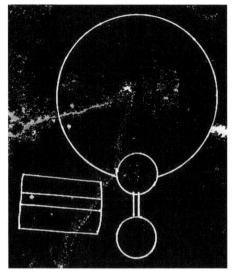

FIG. 33
Drimmies

However, there is another aspect to mirrors. They are magical objects. This is reflected in a great deal of superstition regarding them. The idea that breaking a mirror will bring seven years bad luck is well-known and other practices like turning mirrors after a death in the family suggest ancient, possibly occult belief. This is from Frazer's *The Golden Bough*;

> We can now explain the widespread custom of covering up mirrors or turning them to the wall after a death has taken place in the house. It is feared that the soul, projected out of the person in the shape of his reflection in the mirror, may be carried off by the ghost of the departed, which is commonly supposed to linger about the house till the burial.
>
> 1911, III p.94

This is hardly a Christian idea and may be some sort of pagan survival. Other equally occult beliefs concern the use of mirrors for divining, something mentioned by Chaucer in *The Squire's Tale* and by Burns in his great poem '*Halloween*' where the object was to detect one's future spouse. Like a lot of Halloween customs that were concerned primarily with romance by the late 18th century, it seems likely that these practices once had more serious intent. There are also incidents in the British Isles of it being thought dangerous for a baby to look in a mirror until it reached a year old and it being unlucky for a bride to see herself in a mirror once fully dressed for her nuptials (*Dictionary of Superstitions* p.253). All of these beliefs hint at a fading belief in the magic, if not occult power, of the mirror, and may represent some lost beliefs from pagan times.

Notched rectangle

This symbol occurs in two distinct forms on symbol stones. The symbol referred to in ECMS as the notched rectangle with curved end has been called 'the tuning fork' and has been widely interpreted as a broken sword [FIG. 34]. Given that there is widespread evidence of votive deposits containing broken weapons, tools and other

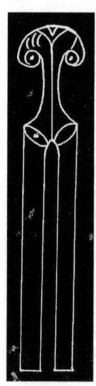

FIG. 34
Dunrobin

domestic objects, and the fundamental warrior aspect of Pictish society, this is surely worth considering. Another interpretation has suggested that the rectangle and Z-rod [FIG. 35] is a representation of a deconstructed chariot. Although Tacitus does tell us of the native tribes using chariots in the 1st century CE there is another possible interpretation of this symbol. Given the emphasis herein on the idea of continuity with earlier people, specifically the ancestors, I think the notched rectangle can be seen as a diagrammatic representation of a chambered tomb. The rectangle has a notch that corresponds to the central chamber and the semi-circles attached to the notch may well refer to the side chambers that lie off the central chamber. If so this could explain the other circles within the body of the rectangle as secondary burials which are known to have taken place in such structures. The Z-rod in this case may be related to some aspect of the heavens, as the chambered tombs are not only rooted in the earth but the majority of the remains

of those represented by the skulls and
thigh bones collected in the tombs had
returned to the earth either through
cremation or burial. If Hutton's idea of the
rituals at such tombs (1991, p.36), that
the community is seeking the blessing of
the ancestors on the planted seeds is
correct, then the significance of such places
would make them a possible candidate for
having a symbol that could be used on the
stones, particularly if, as suggested, the
carving of symbols was rooted in the far past. Just because the
carvers of these stones were expert at depicting animal and everyday objects should not lead us to conclude that they were incapable
of abstract thought. The use of the symbols themselves on standing
stones, bedrock, cave walls and portable objects suggests a widespread
awareness of their meaning and thus a long history of stylisation and
refinement. If they could develop the notched rectangle as a representation of a deconstructed chariot they were surely capable of creating
a diagrammatic representation of a chambered tomb. It is a matter
of which would be the more likely within the mindset of contemporary society.

FIG. 35
Clynemilton

Circular Disc and Rectangle

These occur in two forms, one of which has a notch in the rectangle
[FIGS. 36, 37]. Properly, the parts of these symbols below the circles
have curved sides and are not really rectangles. There is an interpretation that would make some sense. Just as the notched rectangle
may represent chambered tombs it is worth considering whether or
not these circles and rectangles represent brochs. Brochs were built
for around 200 years at the beginning of the Common Era. While
some historians still insist this is too early for them to be called
Pictish, there is no doubt that the people who raised them were
the direct ancestors of those we call the Picts. This means they
were part of the cultural inheritance of the Pictish tribes and as

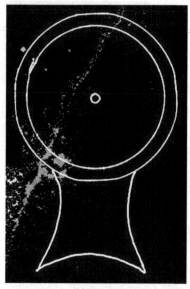

FIG. 36
Inverurie

generations of historians and archaeologists have emphasised the superb practicality of these dry-stone buildings, it is fair to assume that their makers knew just how amazing these structures were. They are reflective of superb architectural thinking, followed by considerable community effort in creating them. They would be something of a treasure to the communities who created them and as such, even if out of use, would have impressed subsequent people with the talents of their ancestors. It is impossible to be sure, but if the areas directly in front of the entry into the broch were used for either practical or even ritual purposes, this could account for the 'rectangles'. It is notable that those circular symbols with notched rectangles all come from

FIG. 37
Sandside

north of Inverness where brochs are most common. The ones without the notch are generally northern too, with several from Aberdeenshire and the only southern example being at Meigle. Again because of the modern world's insistence on the difference between the sacred and the profane, we can be led into not realising that for our ancestors, such differences were likely to have been meaningless, or so intertwined as to have little bearing on their thinking. Thus the practical can exist alongside what we perceive of as the spiritual. Because we can recognise so much of what the Picts carved on their stones, we should perhaps think of the possibility of diagrams for something as complicated but physically massive and obvious, as a chambered tomb or a broch. The idea that some of the symbols may be related to the design of built structures has been considered by Williams (2007, pp.154–6).

Spiral

Allen and Anderson in ECMS have a section on the often intricate spiral decoration on the later stones (1993, I, p.384ff) but there is evidence that the spiral was used in earlier periods. The symbol on the carved fragment at Eday, Orkney [FIG. 38], echoes the much older use of a spiral from Achnabreck, Kilmartin in Argyll [FIG. 39]. This symbol was in use in the British Isles thousands of years before the Pictish period and can be seen at New Grange in Ireland, in other cup-and-ring sites in Argyll, and many other locations. The spiral

FIG. 38
Eday

has been interpreted in many different cultures as being associated with the Mother Goddess. The sites in Argyll may be of some importance here. They are thickest around the Kilmartin Valley, a place where there are a considerable number of prehistoric monuments from a variety of periods. This would suggest an ongoing continuum, if not of specific belief, then certainly of an idea of the area being sacred over a considerable time. We have already noted that there is often a remarkable simplicity or practicality inherent in early symbolism. The plain of Kilmartin looks out to the most remarkable geophysical event in Europe – the Corryvreckan whirlpool. This whirlpool is formed by the Atlantic waters surging round the islands of Scarba and Jura and being forced into the narrow Gulf of Corryvreckan where an underwater spike creates the whirlpool effect. The whirlpool rises from beneath the waves and the

FIG. 39
Achnabreck

spiral shape on the surface is forced out into the oncoming Atlantic tide, whenever the tide is running! The force this requires is truly remarkable and when the tide is at its heaviest in late autumn the whirlpool becomes particularly active. At any time it creates a remarkable booming noise but at this time of the year such is its force that it can sometimes be heard as much as 30 miles away. At this point, the whirlpool is said to form a deep cauldron in the water. I have never seen this but I have seen the waves break from a flat sea, heard the booming noise, and have seen a literal wall of water rising above the sea surface from nearby. To this day, the whirlpool is known in Gaelic tradition as the breath of the Goddess under the Waves and the spike itself is called *An Cailleach*.

One of the stories told of this astounding place is that the name comes from *Coire bhreacain*, the Cauldron of the Plaid, and it is here that the Cailleach, the Goddess in her winter aspect, comes to wash her plaid at the end of autumn. This is said in the story to be what causes the whirlpool at its wildest. After washing her plaid, the traditional one-piece garment of the Highland peoples, she lays it out to dry on Ben Nevis and the Mamore mountains. As she is the oldest creature on earth, the first-born, her plaid is pure white and this is the ancient, mythic explanation for the whirlpool and the first fall of winter snow. It is impossible to believe that early peoples in Argyll did not know of this geophysical wonder, and they would have been impressed by the spirals flowing out into the oncoming Atlantic tide. I have suggested elsewhere (McHardy 2001 and 2002) that people who saw all life as interlinked, as seems to have been the case in pre-Christian times, and who worshipped the Mother Goddess, would see such geophysical events as directly caused by the Goddess herself.

It is therefore worth considering whether the sacredness of the spiral symbol was suggested in the first place by this remarkable geophysical event. Some scholars have suggested that the name Corryvreckan was transposed here from the tidal race of the Aran islands, but a comparison between the two shows the senselessness of that idea, based as it is on the erroneous assumption that Scottish culture was inherited from Ireland. It is after all one of only seven major whirlpools on the planet. We have already seen that the symbol of the cauldron is associated with fertility and regeneration and it is only since humans broke free of the planet's gravity that we have come to realise that there are great eddies in the ocean that act like whirlpools and draw life-sustaining nutrients from the upper warm waters down into the cold depths to sustain life there; an actual case of fertility in practice.

It is also worth considering whether the ancient sacred landscape of nearby Kilmartin Glen is located precisely where it is because of its proximity to the whirlpool. If so, the link between later Pictish symbol carving and the cup-and-ring markings that proliferate particularly in this part of Argyll may well be quite direct, specifically through the associated symbol of the deer (supra).

Z-rod

Some people have gone along with the idea of the broken arrow above and suggested the Z-rod is a broken lance, or spear [FIG. 40]. Again, the ends of this design are differentiated in a fashion that may refer to diurnal time. However, there is another interpretation which fits quite well. This interprets the Z-rod as a lightning bolt. Lightning is very powerful and was seen by many cultures as both a symbol of godhead and of great energy. The druids are supposed to have believed that lightning caused mistletoe to grow on oak trees. The concept of the lightning fertilising trees or even the earth itself is a truly ancient one indeed and we should remember that many ancient participants in sacred rites carried out their rituals on hill-tops – being as near as possible to the sky was clearly significant. One particularly striking Pictish symbol is the Serpent and Z-rod

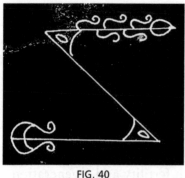

FIG. 40
Detail – Z-rod

[FIG. 1] and as the Serpent has strong chthonic associations, at some level potentially representing the earth itself, this makes a striking symbol when associated with lightning coming from heaven. This might be a symbol of a unison of the forces of the earth and sky representing the creation of life, along the lines suggested by Frazer in *The Golden Bough*, (1978) with a sky god and an earth goddess. We might also think here of the role of the Cailleach as the controller of storms, something which remained associated in popular tradition with witches well into the 19th century. As already noted, symbols in the pre-literate world may well have been multivalent, capable of a range of interpretations, and another aspect of cosmology in general is that it too is not prescriptive in the sense of mathematical formulae. The idea of duality of goddesses in Bride and the Cailleach does not rule out the possibility of a duality of male and female coexisting in belief. In our modern world with our increasing reliance on ever more sophisticated technology we are in danger of underestimating our ancestors because of their lack of technology. For much of humanity's time on this planet our ancestors were just as capable of sophisticated and complex thinking as we are.

Only three symbols are associated with the Z-rod: the serpent, the notched rectangle and double disc. The suggestions here that the serpent is representative of a goddess, specifically Bride, Goddess of Summer, and that the notched rectangle can be construed as representative of a chambered cairn raises ideas which can be seen as supportive of the idea of the Sky Father and Earth Mother. In particular Bride, through the association with the serpent, is clearly linked to chthonic powers and her clear role as a fertility goddess would correspond to this idea, as the plants which feed animals, and humans, grow from the earth. The idea that chambered cairns were the foci of specific ancestor rites asking the spirits of the ancestors to effectively influence the seeds planted in the ground can be seen as related. However, the link with the double discs is more problematic in that I have suggested them to perhaps be, or to include, the concept of a bi-seasonal year. Here one might actually see the Z-rod as symbolic of the weather throughout the year and thus of the goddess herself – she creates the weather in all seasons, winter's storms and cold as the Cailleach, and summer's sun and gentle rain as Bride.

As we shall see, the notched rectangle symbol may itself be closely linked to both the chthonic powers of the earth itself and to the ancestors.

CHAPTER SEVEN

Pre-Christian Religion
in Scotland

SO FAR IN THE analyses of the symbols I have shown recurrent similarities to other societies where the symbols are linked in some way to the feminine principle, if not directly to the idea of a goddess of some kind. We must now look to see if there is evidence that would support the concept of a goddess-centred spirituality in Scotland in the pre-Christian period.

The term pagan is one that has been generally used to describe the beliefs of people before the advent of Christianity, both in Scotland and elsewhere. According to the OED a pagan is: 'One of a nation or community which does not hold the true religion, or does not worship the true God, a heathen.' This of course is a Christian viewpoint, and like followers of most other religions the Christians are certain that theirs is the only true God. This is of some import-ance as all establishment scholarship in Great Britain is rooted in this idea of the truth of Christianity. And it should be remembered that in Scotland our universities were essentially created to train ministers of the Christian religion and not as research centres of objective truth. In terms of the study of the Symbol Stones it is of some interest that the title of Allen and Anderson's ground-breaking study was *The Early Christian Monuments of Scotland*. We have seen that many of the Class I stones, by their classification, can be understood as being rooted in beliefs that were long held here when the Christian missionaries arrived. The OED points out that the original use of the term pagan was associated with beliefs in small communities, and though the term is pretty vague, the idea of locality has much to commend it. While there may have been some sites of particular importance that were known by people over a considerable area, amongst tribal peoples we should be considering localised evidence for ritual and belief. The veneration of trees and sacred groves was widespread in the ancient world (Ross 1967, p.60ff) and the importance of the standing stones and stone circles is well attested. The numbers and distribution of these suggests that ritual and belief were significantly localised, in contrast to the hierarchic Christian religion which had as its centre a city in a country far away from where most of its adherents lived. Such local-isation suggests that surviving evidence for pre-Christian beliefs would itself be widespread. And it is.

A Decayed Goddess

As we have seen in a range of stories from Gaelic oral tradition we meet the Cailleach, often portrayed as a hag or witch who is precisely matched in Scots tradition by the Carlin. Where Gaelic has the *Cailleach Bheur* or biting hag associated specifically with winter, Scots has the Gyre Carlin. Both of these creatures are said to have been landscape formers (MacKenzie 1935, Chs VII, VIII) – they created the known environment – a function of godhead in all human societies. Just as the Christians have the story from their Bible of God creating the world in seven days, our indigenous traditions have the Cailleach and the Carlin creating our landscape. There is, however, a crucial difference. In Scottish tradition these female figures are creating specific, named and known parts of the landscape. The Cailleach was said to have gone about with a great pannier of rocks and earth creating the landscape to her liking. The following is from Hugh Miller's *Scenes and Legends of the North of Scotland*:

> When standing on the site of the huge Ben Vaichaird, the bottom of the pannier is said to have given way, and the contents, falling through the opening, produced the hill, which owes its great height and vast extent of base to the accident.
>
> 1835, p.30

A similar tale was told to explain the creation of the Hebrides. The Carlin is also said to have formed specific spots in the landscape. In a poem attributed to the 15th century we find the following:

Quhill Blaour bled ane quart
Off milk pottage. Inwart
The carling luche and lut fart
North Berwick Law.

Watson, 1995, p.141

The last two lines meaning, 'The Carlin laughed and let fart North Berwick Law' [FIG. 41]. This is a bit bawdy but clearly refers to the Carlin as maker of the landscape, showing her to be, essentially, a goddess. Donald Mackenzie tells us that the Cailleach is indeed the first-born, the oldest being and this too is something we can only understand to be an attribute of godhead:

She shaped the mountains, gave origin to rivers, lochs and marshes, and had a sea connexion; she was the protector of fish and wild animals, whose forms she could assume; and she was connected with uncultivated trees, and was possessed of a magic wand with which she controlled the weather during the winter and spring; she was an enemy of man, but yet a mother of many children; and she had a boulder or standing-stone form. The outwitting of her by means of clever repartee appears to be a memory of incantations and charms which protected human beings and compelled her to render service.

1935, p.174

In many instances the Cailleach and the Carlin are associated with mountains or prominent hills. Many of these hills, like Schiehallion or both the Lomond Hills in Fife, are shaped like the female breast. All over Scotland we have similarly shaped hills called Paps, and sometimes they exist as peaks on larger massifs. Although we find

FIG. 41
North Berwick Law

the term Pap within what were predominantly Gaelic-speaking areas there is a specific Gaelic term with the same meaning *Cioch*, which like Pap means breast or nipple. Some of the most outstanding physical locations in Scotland are called paps, like the East and West Lomond Hills – the Paps of Fife [FIG. 42] – or Arthur's Seat at Edinburgh, like North Berwick Law [FIG. 41], one of the Paps of Lothian – and in Aberdeenshire we have Bennachie [FIG. 43], origi-

FIG. 42
Paps of Fife

nally *Beinn a Ciochan* the Hill of the Pap – its noticeably protuberant peak is called Mither Tap [Mother Top], and was perhaps known in the past as Mither Pap. Another similar site is Lochnagar on Deeside which used to be called *Beinn a Ciochan* too, and which has two significant sites, Meikle

FIG. 43
Bennachie

(Big) Pap and Little Pap. Other similarly shaped and named hills and mountains are the Eildon Hills [FIG. 44] in the Borders, the Paps of Jura [FIG. 45], and Maiden Pap in the Borders and Sutherland. Tinto Hill, an ancient site of fire ceremonies in Lanarkshire has Pap Craig, directly beside Wallace Seat, Wallace here referring to William Wallace, revered as a heroic defender of the Scots against the invading English since the end of the 13th century. The significant figures associated with specific sites appear to sometimes change according to alterations in contemporary culture.

These sites almost all have clusters of what can be interpreted as relevant place names, wells, ancient monuments and stories from the oral tradition. Two examples should suffice to illustrate this. Lochnagar which has both a Meikle and a Little Pap, has a well at the foot of Meikle Pap which used to be called the Well of the White Stones, a stream called *Allt-na-Cailleach* and a lesser peak known as *Casteal na Cailleach*, literally the Cailleach's Castle. The Glen which runs below all of these locations is Glen Muick, from Gaelic

FIG. 44
Eildon Hills

FIG. 45
Paps of Jura

Muc, meaning pig, which as we have seen is in itself significant. On the northern edge of the massif is *Creag nam Ban*, the Rock of the Women, which is reminiscent of the similarly named *Clach na Bhan* further north on Ben Avon, described here by James Porter,

> Walter Gregor mentions Clach-na-bhan, a huge granite rock on top of Meall-na-gaineimh [sandy hill], on the east side of Glenavon. Clach-na-bhan is shaped like an armchair. Women about to be mothers climbed the hill and seated themselves in the hollow believing this ensured them an easy delivery In 1836 a report described the chairing of as many as 'twelve full-bodied women who had that morning come from Speyside, over twenty miles, to undergo the operation'
>
> Porter, 1998

The rock was said also to have the power to bring husbands to single women. Sadly there are no stories I have found about Lochnagar and the Cailleach perhaps due to the 19th century clearances of the local people from the area to create Victorian hunting estates on the lands of their ancestors.

A parallel to this fertility ritual is the Maiden Bore Cave on the northeastern slope of West Lomond Hill, one of the Paps of Fife. Small, writing in 1823 tells us,

> There is a cluster of free stone rocks which jut out from under the base of the hill close beside it, with a large perforation through the rock called the Maiden-bore, because maidens only were supposed capable of passing through it.
>
> Small 1823, p.94

This sounds like a fertility rite akin to one described at the Auld Wives' Lifts in the Kilpatrick Hills in MacDonald's *Rambles Round Glasgow* (1854 URL). The Auld Wives' Lifts are a heap of three massive boulders which in tradition were placed there by three old women from the surrounding district. The rocks sit in a natural amphitheatre and there are cup-and-ring markings in the immediate area, while local folklore suggests this was a 'Druidic' site. There is a hole in the rock outcrop through which young women used to pass in order to ensure fertility. Intriguingly, the Auld Wives' Lifts have a series of 'Celtic' type heads carved on the rocks which were only noticed within living memory.

Higher up from the Maiden Bore Cave on the north east slope of West Lomond Hill, one of the Paps of Fife, is Maiden Castle, a natural outcropping which has no defensive value at all. In the valley to the north is Strathmiglo and its Pictish Symbol Stone with a deer's head, possibly a mask, on it. The general sanctity of the area may well be underlined by the early Christian symbol of the *vesica piscis* on a cluster of rocks between East and West Lomond Hills which was perhaps an attempt to sanctify the area for the new religion along the lines of Pope Gregory's letter to Bishop Mellitus. There is also the Pulpit Rock in Glen Vale on the southern slopes of West Lomond Hill and to its south, a natural stone pillar with its story of a local witch, Carlin Maggie, being turned into the pillar by the Devil (Carlin URL). The association of the Carlin and the Maiden in this area can be seen as conforming to the duality of Cailleach and Bride suggested above. East of West Lomond Hill near the *vesica piscis,* is Maiden Castle, then East Lomond Hill itself, marked on the os maps as a fort and where a Pictish Symbol Stone showing a bull was found. Further to the south is the Sleeping Giant on Benarty Hill, which also has a series of intriguing ancient monuments, wells etc and it seems possible, if not likely, that this Sleeping Giant may well have been perceived as a reclining Goddess. Certainly from the north the figure seems more female than male. In this regard we should also consider the Sleeping Warrior of Arran. From the Isle of Cumbrae, the hills of Arran show a reclining figure which not only has a breast, but appears to have a swollen belly, redolent of a pregnant woman. As such this is another potential Goddess in the landscape.

Bennachie in Aberdeenshire, *Beinn a Cioch*, also has Maiden associations with both the Maiden Causeway on its summit and the

Class II Maiden Stone close by to the north east. The story told of the Maiden stone, where a bride flees from the Devil the night before her wedding to be turned to stone to escape his clutches, is clearly Christian and may well be another instance of assimilating earlier belief and practice into Christian mores. There is a local story concerning a giant Lang Johnny Moir and significantly the place-name Craigshannoch, the second part of which, appears to be the same as shannack – A Halloween bonfire ((The Concise Scots Dictionary 1985 p.605) Shannach, is and thus a direct reference to the fires of Samhain, or Halloween (Jamieson 1882, IV, p.193). This again is redolent of the Lomonds, for, as Watson wrote:

> ... Lomond... is primarily the beacon hill. The Lomond Hills in Fife are, of course, also 'beacons,' and one has only to look at the peaks of the east and West Lomond to see how well suited they were for that purpose.
>
> Watson 1993, p.212

Such beacon hills are well attested to have been used at the old feast days of Beltane and Samhain and possibly include Ben Lomond, which from certain angles is pap-shaped and is the dominant mountain of the area. In Loch Lomond there is the island called Inchcailloch which contains a small hill called *Tom na Nighean*, the Knoll of the Maidens, and there is a traditional story that has a priest killing a nun for breaking her vows of chastity which is itself reminiscent of the supposed sinful behaviour of the Nuns on Priory Island in Loch Tay, who may well have been a group of Nine Maidens, pagan priestesses who appear to have existed in many parts of the world and who are linked to both the Cailleach and Bride (McHardy 2003, *passim*).

I am not the only one to have noticed the significance of the Paps. In his remarkable analysis of Robert Henryson's classic poem *The Twa Mairit Weemen an the Wedo*, the Australian poet Alexander Hope suggests that the activities of the three women are linked to a fairy cult surviving into 15th century Scotland. I think it safe to say that, if there is merit to his analysis, calling it a fairy cult may be underestimating what was going on. He makes the point,

> The shapes of certain hills may by themselves suggest such names as the Maiden-pap in Perthshire or the Hill with the Paps (Bennachie) in Aberdeenshire. But the Paps of Anu in Kerry remind us that not only were such hills sometimes named for their likeness to breasts but because they were thought to be the breast of a Goddess.
>
> 1971, p.37

The idea that such hills were perceived of as the breasts of a Goddess may be rooted in the idea that the world itself was created by a Mother Goddess and therefore if she drew attention to herself in the landscape in such a way, then such sites would be understood as being significant. In Scotland we have some other remarkable breast-shaped hills. The Paps of Jura from the north are remarkably life-like as are the Eildon Hills from the same direction and from certain points on the south bank of the river Clyde the cleft rock of Dumbarton also looks like a pair of female breasts [FIG. 46]. There is a story of the Cailleach associated with the westernmost of the Paps of Jura which explains the scar in the hillside known as *Sgurr na Caillich*. In the story she is a powerful witch-like creature and it was here in the story of Mac Iain Direach (Campbell 1994, Vol 2) that the Seven Big Women of Jura are thrown to their deaths. And the Eildon Hills, a significant prehistoric site, are the location of the well-known story of warriors sleeping inside the hill under the watchful eye of Thomas the Rhymer himself. And while the Paps of Jura have no ancient monuments, the Eildons are rich in ancient artefacts as well as significant place-names and stories that clearly hark back to ritual activity here. That this idea of the Goddess's breast or breasts was widespread can be seen in the further Maiden Paps in the Borders, Sutherland, Kilpatrick Hills and south-west of Dumfries. Interestingly Schiehallion, the central Perthshire mountain that can be seen from Edinburgh on clear days, had this written about it in 1772,

Fortunately, however Perthshire afforded us a remarkable hill, nearly in the centre of Scotland, of sufficient height, tolerably detached from other hills, and considerably larger from east to west than from north to south, called by the people of the low country Maiden-Pap, but by the neighbouring inhabitants Schiehallion, which I have since been informed signifies in the Erse language Constant Storm; a name well adapted to the appearance which it so frequently exhibits to those who live near it, by the clouds and mists which usually crown its summit.

FIG. 46
Dumbarton Rock
[Creative Commons © Dave Hitchborne]

Schiehallion URL

The more generally accepted translation of the name Schiehallion is 'Fairy Hill of the Caledonians' (Watson 1983, p.21). However, the description of the fairy gathering on Schiehallion from Ferguson's Rambles in Breadalbane makes the connections quite explicit:

Here they used to assemble in large numbers and hold their annual convocation, presided over by the beautiful and accomplished Queen Mab, gorgeously arrayed in her favourite green silk robes, with her abundant crop of beautiful golden-yellow hair waving in long ringlets over her shoulder down to her waist. It is said that there are a long series of mysterious caves, extending from one side of the mountain to the other.' Queen Mab, the Queen of the Fairies, was none other than the Cailleach, the Mother Goddess.

1891, p.99

Inadvertently Masklyne also hints at one of the underlying ideas behind the Cailleach as the veiled one, in his reference to its 'misty summit'.

The goddess in the landscape, however, is not restricted to breast shapes alone. To the south of the complex of megalithic sites of Calanais is a line of hills known locally as *Cailich a mointich* – the old woman of the moors. It is here that the moon rises in the same place on consecutive nights at the end of its 18.6 year cycle and on which the main avenue of the stones focusses. Calanais is one of the world's most intriguing megalithic sites and there seems little doubt that the central complex was set up to align with the moon cycle. Linguists reject the possibility of a link between Calanais and the Cailleach but there is evidence to suggest there might be some connection. This comes from the Rhinns of Galloway where on the south-east there is a point called Calliness. That this is not coincidental may be argued from the fact that this promontory contains several ancient monuments, early church sites, the potentially significant place-name Kirkmaiden and what is referred to as a Motte but which, like most such sites, is likely to be a prehistoric mound, whether or not it was used in medieval times. 'Moot' in English like '*moid*' in Gaelic signifies a meeting place, often just such a hill, and is related to similar words in the Scandinavian languages. On the coast nearby is St Medan's Chapel, associated in folklore with Modwenna, who as I have noted elsewhere appears be linked to the initially prehistoric Nine Maidens (McHardy 2003, p.43f) themselves associated with both the Cailleach and Bride (Ibid., *passim*). Mackinlay (1914, p.122) mentions that there was also a chapel near Kirkmaiden dedicated to Bride. This appears to be another cluster of significance which suggests a potential link between Calanais and Cailiness in that both were areas of significant pre-Christian ritual activity. That the names might be purely coincidental I leave to the reader to decide.

Many traditional tales of the Cailleach associate her with mountains, often, like Lochnagar, Ben Cruachan or Ben Wyvis, the highest peak in any particular area and as Mackenzie pointed out (1935, p.142f.) one of the principal roles of this ancient goddess figure was as a weather creator. Prominent peaks are often the focus of weather changes, particularly the onset of storm and blizzard. In this respect the Cailleach's name is of specific interest. It is generally interpreted as meaning 'the veiled one', a singularly apt name for many Scottish mountains which are often shrouded in mist and clouds.

In a range of stories the Cailleach is linked in story to Bride, who was originally a pagan fertility goddess and became a popular figure in the Christianity of the Scottish Highlands. McNeill tells of the relationship between the Cailleach and Bride,

> Another legend shows the Cailleach and Bride not as two contending personalities, but as one and the same. On the Eve of Bride, the Cailleach repairs to the Isle of Youth in whose mysterious woods lies the Well of Youth. There, at the first glimmer of dawn, before any bird has sung or any dog barked, she drinks of the water that bubbles in a crevice of a rock, and having renewed her youth, emerges as Bride, the fair young goddess at the touch of whose wand the dun grass turns to vivid green, starred with the white and yellow flowers of spring.
>
> Ibid., p.21

This, I suggest, makes the Cailleach/Bride a dual goddess whose origins lie in the far past. Dualism has been noted in the Roman references to the Maetae and Caledonii, the division of the Picts into Northern and Southern Scotland and Jackson in particular saw the pairing of symbols as specifically genealogical references to kin-groups (1993, *passim*). In the combined figure of the Cailleach and Bride, rooted in the far past we see a specific duality that can still be seen in the landscape of Scotland today, one example, of several, being *Rubha Bride* and *Rubha Caillich* at opposite ends of Craighouse Bay on Jura. This duality turns up in various places and stories. In Glen Sannox on Argyll the *Leum na Caillich* – the Step of the Cailleach – is directly opposite *Cioch na-h-oighe* – the Pap of the

Maiden, and on the top of Ben Ledi in the Trossachs is *Cnoc na Cailleach* – Rock of the Cailleach – while below it on the shores of Loch Lubnaig is Kilbride. The idea that the Bride place-names in Scotland are all a result of Irish Christian influence holds no more water than the idea that Dalriada was founded by Ulstermen. Jhone Leslie in his 16th century *Historie of Scotland* was quite specific about this:

> The Scottis, Peychtes, Britanis, Inglismen and Irishmen with sik veneratione in ilk place have honoured S Brigida, that innumerable kirks erected to God, amang them ale, to her, ye sal se; yie and mae to her than to ony of the rest: the Irland men contendes that her haly body thay have with thame in that toune quhilke thay cal Dun, in quhilke place the body of thair Apostle S. Patrik is keipet, our countrey men ascrynes the same Glore unto thame quha thinkes, that hitherto thay have honouret it in the Chanrie of Abernethie, and richtie have done thay think.
>
> 1888, I, p.229

The process of assimilating earlier significant figures into the pantheon of Christian saints appears to have been linked to the specific church policy of taking over pagan sites and the pre-Christian Bride seems also to have been known among the Brigantes of north west England. The southernmost known Pictish Symbols on Trusty's Hill at Anwoth, Dumfries and Galloway, are close to the site of a St Bride's chapel (Mackinlay 1914, p.122), which may have been another case of Christian overlay on earlier belief patterns.

An interesting Irish tale has echoes of the Cailleach/Bride duality. In the story of Eochaid Mugmedon a hero kisses an old hag who has been turned away by his brothers. He awakens to find her changed into a beautiful young woman who tells him that she is in fact the Sovereignty of Ireland (Eochaid URL). This is a clear example of a Mother Goddess as the personification of the land itself and can only have come from pre-Christian thought. The duality of Cailleach and Bride finds echo in other ancient ideas such as that of the two season year – the Time of the Big Sun and the Time of the Little Sun. Given that we can discern something of the beliefs concerning the Cailleach and Bride, directly paralleled by those of the Carlin and the Maiden, it does not take too much of a leap of the imagination to understand why such prominent female breast-shaped peaks could become the focus of beliefs, tales and perhaps even ritual.

As we have seen there are several notable Pap and Cioch place-names in the Scottish landscape but there is another related term. This is Mam, here explained by Drummond in *Scottish Mountain and Hill Names*,

> **màm** (Pronounced ma:m) A breast. Originally meaning simply a breast it came through common usage in mountain names to signify a round-topped hill of that shape. The more rounded *màm* hills are often less conically striking than the *ciochs*...
>
> pp.90–91

He goes on to mention the Mamores, the rolling mountains to the south of Ben Nevis, among others. Perhaps we can interpret the *cioch* sites as representative of the goddess as a young woman with the *mam* sites being more redolent of her in her role as the nurturing mother. It may be stretching a point but this differentiation between the younger and older breast shape can be discerned in the Paps of Fife, the Eildon Hills and Dumbarton Rock. This may reflect the inherent duality of the Bride/Cailleach, Maiden/Carlin figures mentioned earlier but whether this was due to human intervention in the landscape or not is unclear, and on current evidence seems unlikely.

If the population believed in a Goddess who was the mother of all creatures and who had created the earth itself, prominent hills and mountains shaped like the female breast could easily become the foci of such beliefs – as if the goddess had made them to be seen as a representation of herself as a nurturer of life.

As an example of the Carlin being active in the landscape this is from Cromek:

We will close our history of witchcraft with the only notice
we could collect, of a celebrated personage, called the Gyre
Carline; who is reckoned the mother of glamour, and near
akin to Satan himself. She is believed to preside over the
'Hallowmass Rades;' and mothers frequently frighten their
children by threatening to give them to M'Neven, or the
Gyre Carline. She is described as wearing a long gray mantle,
and carrying a wand, which, like the miraculous rod of Moses,
could convert water into rocks, and sea into solid land.
Lochermoss, which extends from Solway sea to Locherbrigg
Hill, was once, according to tradition, an arm of the sea,
and a goodly anchorage for shipping. A proud swell of the
Hallowmass tide, which swept away many steeds from the
Carlin's assembly, so provoked her, that, baring her withered
arm, she stretched over the sea her rod of power, and turned
its high waves into a quagmire! There are still carved beaks,
boats, keels, and other remains of shipping, dug up in the
moss at peat casting time.

1810, pp.292–3

Norse sources have figured extensively this far and there is
another connection worth noting. Jennings (2010) writes of the
ogress figures in Orcadian and Shetlandic traditions which he sees as
essentially deriving from Scandinavian originals. Like their Scottish
counterparts, such figures crop up as landscape shapers (Ibid., p.4).
He makes comparison with both the Cailleach and the Gyre Carlin,
seeing the latter as deriving directly from the Norse *gigra*, or giantess
(Ibid., p.9). What can be said with certainty is that both the Celtic
and Germanic languages in Scotland have retained this idea of a giant
female figure, who, while having become a frightening ogre and/or a
hag, was originally a Mother Goddess figure. Given the new
discussions taking place vis-à-vis the antiquity of both Celtic and
Germanic languages in Britain (Oppenheimer, Scutt) we are perhaps
on safe ground in claiming that these survivals, which have so
much in common, in fact arise from a truly ancient concept, that

may or may not have pre-dated the very existence, or development, of these language groups.

Basses

Earlier we looked at the horse symbol from just beside the Bass at Inverurie.

This is not the only instance of a mound called a Bass and others include eg the two mounds at Dunipace (Dun y Bassas?) near Falkirk, Bass Hill at Dryburgh on the Tweed, believed to have been a Pagan site (Dryburgh Abbey URL), Dunipace or Maiden Castle at Kennoway, Fife and Dunipace at Cambusnethan, by Wishaw, also a mound. It is worth considering whether the name Bass may be linked to the considerable number of Scottish pre-Reformation kirks situated on raised mounds. One of the most striking of these is at St Vigeans by Arbroath with its museum of locally found Pictish Symbol Stones. As we have seen, it was deliberate Christian policy from at least the 7th century to take over the pagan precincts or temples for Christian worship and this could account for the number of churches found on such mounds. Many of the mounds with churches built on them are themselves regularly shaped and might well have initially been natural features that were enhanced because of their perceived sanctity. It is worth considering that, if such mounds did have a ritual function in pagan times, that this might be a deliberate echo of the prominent hills which were themselves redolent of sanctity (McHardy 1999, p.220) – and I would suggest it is also worth considering whether many of the artificial mounds, loosely described as Mottes, might be something more akin to sites of prehistoric ritual activity.

There are other similar mounds referred to in folklore as the *sidhe*, or fairy mounds, many of which were undoubtedly burials of one kind or another. Some such small hills, tumuli etc also seem to have been the sites of ritual activity, particularly at Beltane. In *The Silver Bough*, Marian McNeill deals extensively with Beltane (1959, p.55ff), referring to several instances where the fires were lit on knolls or small hills (Ibid., p.72). In this, are we seeing a localised version of bigger events held on larger and more significant hilltop sites? Such local sites are remembered in place-names like Tullybelton (*tulach*, a knoll) in Perthshire. Given what we know of the process of Christianisation, it seems possible that many of the mounds on which churches were built were already sites of ritual practice and this may well have included the lighting of the Beltane, and Samhain, fires. In his remarkable book *A Midsummer Eve's Dream*, Alexander Hope drew attention to such hills:

> The *Statistical Account of Scotland* makes mention of natural or artificial mounds, usually two in number and often near the church or some other pubic place in almost every parish and in many towns and villages. They were known as laws, law hills, *tom-mhoid* (hill of the court of justice), moats, moot-hills, gallows-hills, gibbet hills. The local legends about them were that there in former times the people met to administer justice, make laws and undertake solemn contracts such as signing or witnessing treaties of peace.
>
> 1970, p.85

He mentions two particular sites in Perthshire, Lawton near Dunsinane and Birnam near Dunkeld. However, it is the wide-spread occurrence of these hills that perhaps is a link to the far past. Many commentators have stressed the dispensing of justice through the medieval Baron Baillie courts at such sites, but the role of such mounds seems likely to have stemmed from tribal times and appears to have had nothing to do with feudal practices. As it has been seen that hilltop sites had much more than a simply military so we should reconsider whether these moot-hills etc were also the locations of a range of communal activities, sacral and social. Hope goes on to tell us,

> Another name for these mounds was the Hills of Peace. As nearly all green hills and artificial mounds were regarded as

fairy dwellings and the fairies themselves were often known
as the People of Peace. It is natural to suppose that they
were chosen for their purpose in order that the fairy people
should share in the pacts and acts of judgement and their
execution, and that these acts should have the solemn authority of the sacred place on which they were performed.

Ibid., p.85

If one substitutes the idea of the ancestors for the fairies here, it
would make absolute sense in tribal terms. Such places were effectively hallowed by long use by the same communities over generations.
The meeting of communities to dispense the law was only one of
the circumstances where such locations would be used. Important
weddings, funerals, the allocation of lands, feasts such as Beltane
and Samhain and a host of other activities that involved the entire
community needed a location, and such places fit the bill. Some of
them may also have been the gathering points for clan warriors
when they were called to battle. The fact that so many of these sites
were later declared to be mottes, by people apparently bent on
showing that Scotland was as much a feudalised country as
England, need not bother us here. What is tantalising is whether
such small, localised sites were part of a system that included much
larger hilltop sites, such as the many mentioned herein. If so, was it
a regular occurrence that every few years people from a wide area,
perhaps a tribally designated area, would gather at such sites,
whereas most years they celebrated the feast days more locally?
Some such were used as clan muster points. The number of sites
suggested by Hope would lead us to think that this may well have
been the case. It is tempting to think that the local mounds may also
have something of the sense of the Pap, the marker of the Goddess
herself, about them. Remembering that the Picts must have shared
a great many ideas with their cousins the Britons of Strathclyde, the
Gododdin of Lothian and the Welsh tribes further south, it is
perhaps significant that in the Mabinogion tale of Pwyll and
Pryderi, Pwyll saw Rhiannon on her magic horse while sitting on a

mound. As Rees and Rees pointed out, whoever sat on this mound, 'would see a wonder or suffer wounds or blows' (1990, p.183). The mound is associated with Annwn, the Otherworld and they go on to tell us,

> In Irish tales, mounds outside courts are scenes of games and visionary encounters which do not belong to the round of mundane existence, and the holding of assemblies on hills and mounds is a commonplace of Irish history.
>
> Ibid., p.184

And I would suggest that such activities are rooted in the ancient communal past. Amongst the Scandinavian peoples, the assembly was often held on a mound, and it is noteworthy that at Uppsala, the scene of the most famous pagan celebrations in Scandinavia, there is a series of mounds. Some of these are certainly burial mounds but the idea of sanctifying a site by burying someone there is not uncommon in many societies.

Pictish Photo Art

THE IMAGES ON the following pages are a selection of specific symbols alluded to in this book.

Glamis Manse Centaur

Newton of Garioch

Burghead

Glamis Manse

Meigle 1

Rhynie 5

Ardross

Strathpeffer

Roseisle

Inverurie 4

Kintore 1

Meigle 22

Meigle 5

Abernethy 1

Kintradwell

Glamis Manse Cauldron

Lindores

Logie Elphinstone

Drimmies

Eday

Ardross

Lindores

Conclusion

WE HAVE SEEN that a variety of the symbols used on the early Pictish Symbol Stones appear to be related to ideas associated with powerful female figures of Celtic, Germanic and other traditions. In Scottish terms she is the Cailleach and the Carlin and it is notable that she is both a weather worker and a landscape creator (Mackenzie 1935, Ch VII) but that she also has the power to bestow life as is shown in the following excerpt from the story of The Knight of the Red Shield:

> She (the Cailleach) came up to the battlefield, and threw two between her and him. She put her finger in their mouths, and she brought them alive; and they rose up whole as best they ever were. She reached him and she put her finger in his mouth, and he snapped if off her from the joint. She struck him a blow of the point of her foot, and she cast him over seven ridges.
>
> 'Thou pert little wretch,' said she,' thou art the last I will next-live in the battle field.'
>
> Campbell 1994, 2, p.85

Here, the Cailleach is explicitly saying she will not use her power to bring anyone else back to life. She clearly has done so before. She has the power of life and death. Given these attributes, it does not seem to be stretching a point to see the Cailleach/Carlin as a decayed Goddess figure. In several of the tales in Campbell's collections the hero fights with a Cailleach, who is always presented as a giant, ugly and fearsome hag. While this may represent the winter aspect of an earlier dual goddess whose summer aspect is that of Bride, the golden fruitful young woman, the hag is a suitable foe for the hero in tales which, whatever their original provenance, by the time

Campbell and his colleagues were collecting them in the 1880s, had been told within a Christian society for hundreds of years. This is the goddess I suggest who was understood as having put the Paps and Ciochs in the landscape, the story of her having 'lut fart' North Berwick Law being a specific, surviving instance of this idea. Likewise, her association with Ben Nevis, Ben Wyvis, Lochnagar, Schiehallion etc which are mountains often veiled in mist, as she herself was veiled, underlines this fundamental relationship with the landscape. WFH Nicolaisen made an interesting point about the P-Celtic place-name *Aber*, a confluence, in Scotland, telling us,

> Although it would be rash to claim that every *aber*-site has cultic origins or unspecified connections with 'river-worship', several of them can be confidently placed in that category.
>
> 1997, p.117

This fits in with the interpretation of localised ritual activities in the landscape, and Nicolaisen makes the link directly with the idea of river-goddesses (Ibid.). The further link with wells and fertility rituals is well attested.

In *A New History of the Picts* I suggest that we should consider the Picts, the first inhabitants of Scotland to be mentioned in written sources, as the indigenous people of this land. There is no evidence to suggest otherwise. This is not to say that they were in any way isolated and separate from the rest of Europe. Over the millennia, people have come and gone but the latest genetic investigations support the idea that a substantial part of our modern survivors are descended, in great part, from the earliest post Ice-Age population. And it was their descendants that the Romans called Picts. They would thus have inherited the traditions and beliefs of their own ancestors and it is this ancient stratum of belief that I suggest underpins the use of the symbols they chose to decorate their Symbol Stones.

Whatever further uses the symbols, and the stones themselves, may have had – as educational tools, as the foci of ritual, as landscape markers and in the post-Christian period, perhaps even as individual memorials – there is ample evidence to support the idea that within the corpus of symbols that have survived, we can discern something of what the Picts believed before the Christians came. And that, I suggest, was rooted in a respect both for the ancestors and for nature, which was perceived as being fundamentally feminine. While I have drawn attention to instances of links between the Cailleach and Bride, Carlin and Maiden, it seems very likely that there was another duality that may still be discernible in Scotland's landscape, that of the Cailleach and the Bodach, or Old Man. A subject to which I hope to return.

In terms of the stones themselves, some Class II and III stones clearly show scenes taken from the Christian Bible, which suggests that the pre-Christian stones themselves had some sort of religious meaning, and that this level of use was carried on by the new religion. That the symbols themselves are not standardised – though recognisable none of them occur even twice exactly the same – emphasises that whatever belief system was associated with the Class I stones, it was localised. There does not appear to be any central point of religious power or control directing how the symbols would, or could, be used. This is what would be expected of a tribal society where the socio-economic power structures were based on kin-group dynamics. The ideas behind the symbols were clearly widespread but the actual execution of them appears always to be rooted in local experience. This echoes what we know of the story-telling process which, in pre-literate times, was of great importance to what we now think of as education. This is not to say that there were no unifying ideas – the suggested importance of specifically shaped hills and mountains would be appreciated over quite wide areas – but that the creation of the earliest symbol stones was something done within the tribal structure of society, based on ideas that were common across all, or most of the tribes. However, all such material would be presented through the oral tradition within the known environment of the localised audience. Given what we know of the occupation of Scotland, such ideas had arisen amongst communities that had been rooted in their particular landscapes for millennia. How old these ideas were is impossible to know but I hope that the suggestions I have made show that not only was there an underlying series of related ideas and beliefs behind the creation of the symbols, but that they were rooted in indigenous experience.

Coda

IN NOVEMBER 2011, after I thought this book was completed, I went out to visit a site in Fife which I have long considered of interest. This was the dolorite stone pillar on the west side of the Lomond Hills above Balgeddie, known in folklore as Carlin Maggie, given on the OS Pathfinder map as Carlin and Daughter. This is close to West Lomond Hill, one of the Paps of Fife, on the north-eastern slope of which is Maiden Castle and on the north side of which is the Maiden Bore Stone. The story of Carlin Maggie is that she was a powerful local witch who made the mistake of taking on the Devil. As a result she was turned into the pillar of stone. All pictures I had seen of this pillar showed a straight, essentially phallic shape. These pictures were taken from the south looking north along the steep slope of Bishop Hill. On making my way there I went past the pillar to view it from the west. There above me was a shape that immediately put me in mind of the pregnant goddess figures which have survived from various parts of Europe [FIG. 47]. While we have no pictures from 1,500 years ago to show what Carlin Maggie looked like then, the combination of a phallic aspect with that of the pregnant goddess (cf. Gimbutas 1996, p.36) is a striking one and would seem to suggest that this may well have been understood as a site of sanctity in the far past. If so the development of local tradition into a tale of a witch scrapping with the Christian devil would not be unexpected. All history and archaeology is dependent on informed guesswork and in this case I

FIG. 47
Carlin Maggie

suggest that this combination of the female and male symbols in one figure is redolent of a male/female symbolic duality that co-existed with the Mother/Maiden duality of the Cailleach and Bride, Carlin and Maiden.

Appendix A

THE FOLLOWING ARE examples of Pap and Cioch sites outlining the variety of potentially supportive evidence for the existence of locations for sacral activities and the foci of pre-Christian belief.

Bennachie

Initially Beinn a Cioch, the hill of the nipple or pap
Craigshannoch, Rock of the Samhain Fire
Maiden Stane
Maiden Causeway
Mither Tap
Stone circles at Chapel of Garioch, Chapel o Sink, East
    Aquhorthies and Hatton of Ardoyne.
Standing stones at Hatton of Ardoyne, Monymusk and Tombeg
Symbol Stones at Logie
Whitecross
Whitewell

Cioch Mhor

The Big Nipple or Pap has a smaller Cioch Bheag, to the northeast. It is in the shadow of Ben Wyvis, itself said to have been created by the Cailleach. A local tale has it that Ben Wyvis is occupied by the Winter Hag who has the maiden of Spring imprisoned.

On the southern and eastern slopes are chambered cairns at Heights of Brae and Balnacrae.
Close by at the eastern end of Knockfarrel is a traditional healing well.

Eildon Hills

Three hills in the borders that from several angles are like a pair of breasts, or Paps. Associated in story with both 'King Arthur' and Thomas the Rhymer.

Eildon means old, suggesting ancient sanctity.

Rhymer's Stone at reputed site of Eildon Tree where Thomas met with Queen of Elfland.

Fort on one summit

St Mary's Well – reports of other wells in earlier times.

Nearby Bass Hill at Dryburgh

Roman signal station on summit and camp nearby

Lochnagar

Initially called Beinn a Ciochan, the Hill or Mountain of the Breasts.
Alltcailleach Forest
Caisteal na Caillich
Carn an t-Sagairt Beg and Mor. Cairns of the Priest
Cnapan Nathraichean, The Knoll of the Adders (Bride or Druidic reference?)
Coire na Ciche, Corry of the Nipple or Pap
Glen and Loch Muick, from Muc, a pig or swine
Little Pap
Meikle Pap
White Mounth

Paps of Fife

East and West Lomond Hill. According to CPNS, Lomond means beacon.
Pictish Symbol Stone of a bull found on East Lomond Hill
Maiden Bower – geophysical feature used in fertility rite
Maiden Castle – not a fortification

The Carlin and her daughter – geophysical feature: Carlin is Scots
    for Cailleach
Devil's Burdens – geophysical feature
Early church site at nearby Orwell
Earthwork in Glen Vale
Early Christian Symbol Stone with fish and cross on W. Lomond
    Hill
Fort on East Lomond Hill

Paps of Jura

Jura is originally Norse and means Deer Isle. The Paps are three
mountains one of which is Beinn Shantaidh, the Holy Mountain.
The others are Beiin an Oir, the Mountain of Gold and Beinn a'
Chaolais, the Mountain of the Sound. On Beinn an Oir, there is
Sgriob na Cailich, a gash on the hillside where a hag is said to have
slid down the side of the mountain. This location is also associated
with the Seven Big Women of Jura, who in tradition had the Glaibh
Soluis, the Sword of Light. They may have originally been nine in
number (see McHardy 2003). The Corryvreckan at the north end
of the island has many Goddess associations and traditions and is
one of the world's seven significant whirlpools. Its spiral shapes,
thrown into the Atlantic Tide are the Breath of the Goddess under
the Waves and may have inspired northern European use of the
spiral motif. On the east of the island at Small Isles Bay there are
Rubha (point) na Caillich and Rubha Bhride and Eilean Bhride.

Paps of Lothian

Used to describe North Berwick Law and Arthur's Seat. North
Berwick Law is a major landmark and linked to 17th century witch
activity. Within living memory stories have been told of Arthur and
his warriors sleeping inside the hill.
Arthur's Seat has St Anthony's Wells which was used for healing
St Anthony's Chapel

A hill fort on the summit

The Slippy Stanes mentioned by Mackenzie (1935, p.263) as a fertility site.

Appendix B

Matriliny

IF MY INTERPRETATION of a Mother Goddess religion amongst the Picts, and their predecessors, is in fact correct than this can be seen as supportive of the much discussed notion of Pictish matriliny. Kyle Gray (PAS Journal 10, pp.7–14, 1996) drew attention to the fact that many of the names of the progenitors of the kings in the Pictish king-lists seem feminine. Gray mentions similar, or cognate, names from Irish and Welsh sources. She compares the Pictish Aniel with the Irish Aine or Anu, Bargoit with Birgit or Brigit and Donuel with the P-Celtic Dôn, all names which are associated with early Goddess figures. Dr Emily Lyle of the School of Scottish Studies put forward a suggestion for a model on which such a matrilineal succession could function (1992). In such a society the king could only attain his position by marrying the queen, the hereditary representative of sovereignty. We know from early Irish sources that the concept of sovereignty being manifested in a female, perhaps even a direct representative of the goddess, was not unknown. In Dr Lyle's model the line of queens was matched by another female line, of women who gave birth to sons, who were eligible to become kings. In one of those resonances that border on the mystical Dr Lyle suggested that cosmologically the line of queens would be seen as yellow and the line of king-mothers as black. This corresponds directly to the idea of Bride, the golden Goddess of Summer and representative of fertility, and the black Cailleach, Hag of Winter.

While we may never be absolutely certain as to the precise meaning, or meanings of the Symbols as used by the Picts – and particularly the Beastie – the idea that they were used within a belief system that encompassed both the idea of a Mother Goddess and a reverence for the ancestors I believe has much to commend it. The past is a foreign country and one for which we have no map and which we can never visit. However, by taking on board the possibilities herein suggested it may be possible to find out more and gain a clearer picture. In a world under threat from a male dominated, exploitative philosophy, we are perhaps in need of something a bit more sympathetic to the planet herself.

Appendix C

The Glamis Manse Stone

Though all Pictish Symbol Stones are unique, the Glamis Manse stone is particularly different from all others. On one side it has simple picked out symbols of a salmon and an adder. The stone itself has been shaped and on the other side is an ornate Christian Cross, conforming to Class II. However, the symbols on the cross-side are striking. Top left below the transverse arm of the cross is a cauldron with two pairs of legs sticking out of it, and below it are two men fighting with what appear to be axes or hammers. On the other side of the stone there is a deer head over a view of a cauldron from above. We thus have two cauldrons. The one on the left I suggest is a specific reference to the idea discussed above of the Cauldron of Regeneration and rebirth. The deer opposite it can be seen as a mask and thus referring to some form of pre-Christian ritual. The cauldron below the deer head may well be a symbol of fertility, and one which I have suggested may be directly linked to the Cailleach, much as the serpent or adder can be linked with Bride. What the two men fighting refer to is unclear, but may have something to do with the duality we have already looked at. Further to this Scotland abounds with stories of giants living on opposite hills fighting with each other, though that fighting is usually restricted to the throwing of giant boulders. The figures on this stone appear to be engaged in some form of ritual combat.

What is clear is that this stone has significant pre-Christian and Christian elements in its execution. It is highly likely that the serpent and adder were carved on a plain standing stone long before the cross and other symbols were added. If so why were the earlier symbols left? Can we see here an example where a stone was being used to accommodate both the pre-Christian and Christian beliefs? Given that the idea that Christianity simply took over all preexisting ritual practice in a peaceful and steady fashion is no more than propaganda. In many parts of the world the process of changing religion has been brutal and bloody and why should we believe Scotland to be any different just because it suits the triumphant Christians to tell themselves this? However, to read the stone as a marker of an ongoing accommodation between two competing philosophies is anything but absurd. And we should remember that the Columban church which was dominant in Scotland before the 664CE Synod of Whitby was a much more locally based and probably locally accountable organisation in a way that the soon to be dominant Church of Rome certainly was not.

Bibliography

Adam, J 1993. *The Declaration of Arbroath* The Herald Press, Arbroath.

Alcock, EA 1989. *Pictish Stones Class I: Where and How?* Glasgow Archaeological Journal 15: 1–21.

Alcock, L 1996. *Ur-Symbols on the Pictograph system of the Picts* Pictish Arts Society Journal 9: 2–5, Edinburgh.

Alexander, W 1877. *Notes and Sketches Illustrative of Northern Rural Life in the Eighteenth Century* David Douglas, Edinburgh.

Allen, JR & Anderson, J 1993 (repr). *The Early Christian Monuments of Scotland* Pinkfoot Press Balgavies, Angus.

Anywl, E 1906. *Ancient Celtic Goddesses* The Celtic Review v III No 9.

Ballochmyle URL http://myweb.tiscali.co.uk/celynog/Scottish/20Islands/ballochmyle_carvings.htm

Banks, M 1937–41. British Calendar Customs 3v Glaisher London

Bede 1955. *A History of the English Church and People*, Penguin, London.

Blackford Hill URL http://www.themodernantiquarian.com/site/6527/blackford_hill.html

Blackhills URL http://canmore.rcahms.gov.uk/en/site/16404/details/blackhills+house/

Brodie, J 1996. *Ancient Pictorial Carvings on Stones in Scotland* Pictish Arts Society Journal (PASJ) 9, Edinburgh.

Britannia URL http://www.britannia.com/history/arthur/kamyth.html

Brown, PWF 1965. *The Luxuriant Pig* Folklore 76 No 4 pp.288–300.

Burt, E 1998 (repr). *Burt's Letters from the North of Scotland* Birlinn, Edinburgh.

Campbell, E 2001. *Were The Scots Irish?* Antiquity Vol. 75 pp.285–292.

Campbell, JF 1994. *More West Highland Tales* Birlinn, Edinburgh.

Campbell, JF 1994 (repr). *Popular Tales of the West Highlands* Birlinn, Edinburgh.

Carlin URL http://www.veg.nildram.co.uk/carlin.htm

Cessford, C 1998. *Tongs and' Tuning Forks* PASJ 13: 4–7, Edinburgh.

Charlotte Guest's Mabinogion http://www.lundyisleofavalon.co.uk/texts/welsh/taliesin.htm

Compact Edition of the Oxford English Dictionary 1979 Book Club Associates, London.

Cromek, RH et al. 1810. *Remains of Nithsdale and Galloway Song* Alexander Gardner, Paisley.

Cummins, WA 1999. *The Picts and Their Symbols* Sutton, Stroud.

Cunliffe, B 2001. *Facing the Ocean* Oxford University Press

Davidson, HRE 1988. *Myths and Symbols in Pagan Europe* Manchester.

Davidson, HRE 1998. *Roles of the Northern Goddess* Routledge, London.

Dio Cassius; trans Cary, E 1927. *Dio's Roman History* Heinemann, London.

Donovan URL http://ftvdb.bfi.org.uk/sift/series/18458

Douglas, S 1987. *The King o the Black Art and other folk tales* Aberdeen University Press.

Driscoll, ST and *Nieke, MR, eds.1988. Power and Politics in Early Medieval Britain and Ireland* Edinburgh University Press.

Drummond, P 1991. *Scottish Mountain and Hill Names* Scottish Mountaineering Trust Nairn.

Dryburgh Abbey URL http://www.scottish-places.info/features/featurehistory6544.html

Eggerness URL http://www.themodernantiquarian.com/site/11230/eggerness.htm

Eliade. M 1989. *Shamanism* Arkana, London.

English URL http://www.archaeology.ws/language.html

Eochaid Mugmedon URL http://www.maryjones.us/ctexts/eochaid.html

Forbes, AP 1874. *The lives of St Ninian and St Kentigern* Edmonston & Douglas, Edinburgh (Historians of Scotland vol v).

Ferguson, M 1891. *Rambles in Breadalbane* Thomas Murray & Son, Glasgow.

Fowler, JM 1943. *False Foundations of British History* Melbourne

Frazer, JG 1978 (repr). *The Golden Bough* MacMillan, London

Friell, JPG and Watson WG (eds.) 1984. *Pictish Studies: Settlement, Burial and Art in Dark Age Northern Britain* BAR, Oxford.

Gimbutas, M 1982. *The Goddesses and Gods of Ancient Europe* Thames & Hudson, London.

Ginsburg, C 1991. *Ecstasies: Deciphering the Witches' Sabbath* University of Chicago Press.

Glen Domhain URL http://www.turnaltfarm.co.uk/deer1.html

Glutton-Brock, J & McGregor, A 1988. *An end to Medieval Reindeer in Scotland* Proceeding of the Society of Antiquities of Scotland (PSAS) 118: 23–35.

Golding, A 1587. *The Excellent and Pleasant Work of Julius Solinius Polyhistor* Thomas Hacket, London.

Graves, R 1961. *The White Goddess* Faber & Faber, London.

Gray, K. 1996. *A new look at the Pictish King List* Pictish Arts Society Journal 10 Edinburgh.

Gundestrup URL http://www.archeurope.com/index.php?page=gundestrup-cauldron

Haldane, ARB 1952. *The Drove Roads of Scotland* Thomas Nelson & Sons, Edinburgh.

Hedges, J 1984. *Tomb of the Eagles* John Murray, London.

Henderson, G 1911. *Survivals in Belief among the Celts* Maclehose & Sons, Glasgow.

Henderson, I 1982: 'Pictish Art and the Book of Kells' in *Ireland in Early Mediaeval Europe: Studies in Memory of Kathleen Hughes*, (ed Whitelock, D McKitterick, R Dumville, D) Cambridge University Press:, pp.79–105.

Hicks, C 1993. *Animals in Early Medieval Art*, Edinburgh University Press.

Hope, AD 1971. A *Midsummer Eve's Dream* Oliver & Boyd, Edinburgh.

Hutton, R 1991. *The Pagan Religions of the ancient British Isles* Blackwell, Oxford.

Isaacs, J 1991. *Australian dreaming; 40,000 years of Aboriginal history* Smith Press, NSW.

Jacobson, E 1993. *The Deer Goddess of Ancient Siberia* E J Brill, New York.

Jackson, A 1984. The *Pictish Symbol Stones of Scotland* Orkney Press, Orkney.

Jackson, A 1993. *Pictish Symbol Stones?* The Association for Scottish Ethnography, Edinburgh.

James, S 1999. *The Atlantic Celts* British Museum Press, London.

Jamieson, JA 1857. *A Dictionary of the Scots Language* Wm Nimmo, Edinburgh.

Jennings, A 2010. *The Giantess as a Metaphor for Shetland's cultural history* Shima: The International Journal of Research into Island Cultures Volume 4 Number 2.

Jones, G & Jones, M 1993. *The Mabinogion* Everyman, London.

Juniper URL http://www.herbal-supplement-resource.com/juniper-herb.html

Kermack, S 1997. *An attempt on the meaning of the Pictish symbols – Part I* PASJ 11 Edinburgh.

Koch, JT 1997. *The Gododdin of Aneurin* University of Wales Press, Cardiff.

Leslie, J 1888–1895 (repr). *Historie of Scotland* Scottish Text Society, Edinburgh.

Lethbridge, TC 1962. *Witches* Routledge and Kegan Paul, London.

Logan, J 1831. *The Scottish Gael,* Smith, Elder and Co, London.

Lyle, E 1992. *A Line of Queens as the pivot of a Cosmology* in *Women and Sovereignty* ed. L Fradenberg, Edinburgh University Press.

Macaulay, A 2006. *Megalithic Measures and Rhythms* Floris Books, Edinburgh.

Macaulay, J 1997. *Mirrors and Mirror Cases* PASJ 11 Edinburgh.

MacDonald, H 1854. *Rambles Round Glasgow* URL http://www.electricscotland.com/history/glasgow/index.htm

McHardy, SA 1999. *Scotland, Myth, Legend and Folklore* Luath, Edinburgh.

McHardy, SA 2001. *The Quest for Arthur* Luath, Edinburgh.

McHardy, SA 2003. *The Quest for the Nine Maidens* Luath, Edinburgh.

McHardy, SA 2004. *School of the Moon* Birlinn, Edinburgh.

McHardy, SA 2005. *Tales of the Picts* Luath, Edinburgh.

McHardy, SA 2010. *A New History of the Picts* Luath, Edinburgh.

Mack, A 1998. *The Association of Pictish Symbols with Ecclesiastical, Burial and 'Memorial' areas* Pinkfoot, Balgavies.

Mackay, JG 1934. *The Deer-Cult and the Deer-Goddess Cult of the Ancient Caledonians* Folklore XLII, London.

Mackenzie, DA 1935. *Scottish Folk-Lore and Folk-Life* Blackie, Glasgow.

Mackenzie, DA 1995 (repr). *Crete and Pre-Hellenic Myths and Legends* Senate, London.

Mackinlay, JM 1893. *Folklore of Scottish Wells and Springs* Wm. Hodge, Glasgow.

McNeill, M 1957–68. *The Silver Bough* 4 vols MacLellan, Glasgow.

Mann, J C 1988. The history of the Antonine Wall – a reappraisal PSAS 118, pp.131–137

Markale J 1986. *Women of the Celts* Inner Traditions International, Vermont.

Miller, H 1890. *Scenes and Legends of the North of Scotland* Nimmo, Hay & Mitchell, Edinburgh.

Nennius: 1980. *The History of Britain* in Arthurian Period Sources ed. J Morris, Phillimore, London.

Nicolaisen, WFH 1997. *On Pictish Rivers and their Confluences* in *the worm, the germ and the thorn* pp.113–19

Opie, I & Tatem, M (eds.) 1989. *A Dictionary of Superstitions* Oxford University Press.

Oppenheimer, S 2006. *The Origins of the British – A Genetic Detective Story* Constable and Robinson, London.

Oxenham, W 2005. *Welsh Origins of Scottish Place-names* Gwasg Carreg Gwalch, Llanwrst, Wales.

Porter, J 1998. *The Folklore of Northern Scotland: Five Discourses on Cultural Representation* Folklore: 109.

Rees, A & Rees, B 1961. *Celtic Heritage* Thames & Hudson, London.

Rennie, JA 1960. *The Scottish People* Hutchison, London.

Reynolds, PJ 1979. *Iron Age Farm: The Butser Experiment* British Museum Publications, London.

Rhys, J 1901. *Celtic Folklore; Manx and Welsh* Frowde, London.

Rolleston, TW 1986 (repr). *Celtic Myths and Legends* Bracken, London.

Ross, A 1993 (repr). *Pagan Celtic Britain* Constable, London.

Sacred Texts URL http://www.sacred-texts.com/neu/celt/cml/cml25.htm

Samson R 1992. *The Reinterpretation of the Pictish Symbols* Journal of the British Archaeological Association, Volume 145: 29-65.

Schiehallion URL http://www.sillittopages.co.uk/schie/schie57.html

Scott, D 2001. *Watchers of the Dawn* CD Tain, contact douglas.scottt@virgin.net

Scott, W 1843. *Manners, Customs and History of the Highlanders of Scotland* Thomas Morison, Glasgow.

Shlain, L 1998. *The Alphabet versus the Goddess* Penguin, London.

Skene, WF 1837. *The Highlanders of Scotland* John Murray, London

Sky Father URL http://en.wikipedia.org/wiki/Sky_father

Small, A 1823. *Interesting Roman Antiquities Recently Discovered in Fife* Edinburgh.

Smyth, AP 1984. *Warlords and Holy Men* Edward Arnold, London.

Sorcerer URL http://www.faculty.umb.edu/gary_zabel/Courses/ Phil281/PhilosophyofMagic/MyDocuments/Therianthropes.htm

Spearman, M & Higgit, J 1992. *The Age of Migrating Ideas* Alan Sutton, Stroud.

Spence, L & Spence, L 1995 (repr). *The Magic Arts of Celtic Britain* Constable, London.

Swan, VG 1999. 'Legio xx Valeria Victrix and the Antonine Wall: new perspectives in the history of Northern Britain' in N. Gudea (ed.) *Roman Frontier Studies 1997, Proceedings of the xviith International Congress of Roman Frontier Studies*, Oxbow Monograph 91, Oxford, 289–294.

Swire, O 1963. *The Highlands and their Legends* Oliver & Boyd, Glasgow.

Tacitus, Mattingly H (ed.) 1948. *Tacitus on Britain and Germany* Penguin, London.

The worm, the germ and the thorn; Pictish and related studies presented to Isabel Henderson 1997 Pinkfoot Press Balgavies, Angus.

Thomas, C 1963. *The Interpretation of the Pictish Symbols* Archaeological Journal 120: 31–97.

Thomas, C 1984. *The Pictish Class I Symbol Stones* in Friell and Watson

Thomas, C 1994. *And Shall These Mute Stones Speak* UWP, Cardiff.

Turville-Petre, EOG 1964. *Myth and Religion of the North* Weidenfeld and Nicolson, London.

Tyndale, A *Animal Masks and Costumes* PASJ 8 Edinburgh.

Wainwright, WF 1955. *The Problem of the Picts* Nelson, London.

Watson, R. (ed.) 1995. *The Poetry of Scotland*, Edinburgh University Press.

Watson, WJ 1994 (repr). *The Celtic Place Names of Scotland* (CPNS) Birlinn, Edinburgh.

Williams. H 2007. Cambridge Archaeological Journal 17(2): 145–64.

Williams, M *Amatheon, Son of Don* URL
http://www.saltpublishing.com/horizon/issues/01/text/williams_mar ko1.htm

Time Line

*c.*18000BCE	Maximum Glaciation of the last Ice Age
*c.*10000BCE	Evidence of human activity at Elsrickle, near Biggar
8500BCE	Settlement at Cramond, by Edinburgh
7500BCE	Shell midden near Applecross
6500BCE	Evidence of tent-like structures on Rum
5000BCE	Monumental refuse heaps – sea shells etc in Hebrides
4000BCE	Domestication of animals
3600BCE	Balbridie near Stonehaven, timber hall built; evidence of agriculture
3500BCE	Temple Wood circle raised in Kilmartin Glen, Argyll
3500BCE	First use of Cairnpapple Hill complex in Lothian
3200BCE	Skara Brae in Orkney first built
3100BCE	Stenness Stone circle in Orkney raised
2900BCE	First circle raised at Calanais, Isle of Lewis
2700BCE	Maes Howe chambered cairn built in Orkney
2500BCE	Ring of Brodgar raised in Orkney
2000BCE	Calva Cairns near Culloden raised
2000BCE	Start of cup-and-ring rock carvings, Achnabreac, Argyll
1500BCE	Bennachie and Traprain Law hilltop sites come into use
1250BCE	First evidence of wheeled transport Blair Drummond Moss
800BCE	Bronze objects found at Corrymuckloch near Crieff
600BCE	Beginning of Atlantic roundhouses
400BCE	Chariot burial at Newbridge near Edinburgh
100BCE	First brochs a begin to appear
55BCE	Romans land in southern Britain
43CE	Claudius invades Britain
70–80	Romans come to Scotland; Gask ridge forts built
74	Rebellion of the Brigantes
81	Supposed Battle of Mons Graupius; Calgacus and Caledonian Confederation
85	Fort at Inchtuthil abandoned
108	Roman positions north of Tyne-Solway destroyed
122–36	Building of Hadrian's Wall
143–8	Building of Antonine Wall
150	Compilation of Ptolemy's Geography
150–54	Brigantes rise again

164	Antonine Wall abandoned
180–5	Hadrian's Wall overrun
208	Remanning of forts on Hadrian's Wall by Septimus Severus
210	Defeat of the Maetae
211	Death of Severus, Roman withdrawal to Hadrian's Wall
215	Last legionary fort in Caledonia, Carpow abandoned
297	First surviving literary use of the term Picts
306	Constantine proclaimed Roman emperor at York; frontier consolidated
310	Mention of Caledonians and other Picts
367	Barbarian Conspiracy overruns Hadrian's Wall
368	Ammianus says Picts are Dicalydones and Verturiones
387	Roman garrisons leave frontier
400	Germanic-speaking mercenaries consolidate Northumbria
407	Last Romans leave Britain
405–500	Earliest Christian cemeteries, Whithorn and Kirkmadrine, are established
500	Floruit of Ninian, Fergus mac Erc dies
525–550	Bernicia formed by Angles centred on Bamburgh
563	Columba exiled to lands in Alba
570	Floruit of Ryderch Hen of Strathclyde
570–600	Floruit of Kentigern
574	Columba ordains Aedan Mac Gabhran, king of Dalriada
585	Death of Bridei mac Maelchon
590	Urien of Rheged killed at siege of Lindisfarne
593–617	Northumbrian expansion under Ethelfrith
c.600	Gododdin raid
603	Aedan mac Gabhran beaten at Degastan by Ethelfrith
c.608	Aedan dies
617	Martyrdom of St Donnan on Eigg
617–33	Edwin becomes king of Northumbria. Oswald and Oswiu xiled amongst Picts and Scots
629–42	Domnall Brecc king of Scots
634–41	Oswald king of Northumbria
634–51	Bishop Aidan controls Northumbrian church
638	Northumbrian assault on Edinburgh
641–70	Oswiu king of Bernicia and from 655 of Northumbria
653–57	Talorcan son of Eanfrith king of Picts
660–80	Northumbrian conquest of Rheged

664	Synod of Whitby
670–85	Ecgfrith king of Northumbria
672	Drest deposed and Picts massacred by Ecgfrith
679	Adomnan Abbot of Iona
681	Anglian bishopric at Abercorn
685	Battle of Dunnichen
685–705	Aldfrith king of Northumbria
688–92	*Life of Columba* written
c.700	Re-establishment of Eigg
70d	Adomnan dies
706–24	Nechtan mac Derile king of Picts
711	Picts slaughtered by Saxons in plain of Manaw
717	Nechtan expels Columban clergy
729–61	Oengus i king of Picts
750	Eadbeht of Northumbria conquers Kyle
750–2	Teudubr, son of Bili, king of Strathclyde rules Picts
780–6	*Book of Kells* begun on Iona
793	Viking raid on Lindisfarne
795	Vikings lay waste Skye and Iona
802	Vikings attack Iona again
807–14	New church at Kells for Iona *familia*
811–20	Constantine son of Fergus, king of Dalriada and Picts
820–34	Oengus ii, son of Fergus king of Dalriada and Picts
839	Major Viking victory over Picts
840	Kenneth MacAlpin king of DalRiata
c.847	Kenneth king of Scots and Picts
850–70	Viking domination of the west
858–62	Donald i king of Picts and Scots. Laws of Dalriada read at Forteviot
862	Constantine king of Picts and Scots
866–7	Danes conquer Northumbria
866–9	Olaf the White attacks the Picts
870–90	Migration of Scottish Vikings to Iceland
875	Halfdan attacks Picts and Britons of Strathclyde
877	Aed king of Picts and Scots
878–	Giric, last king of Picts
900	Scots annex Strathclyde

List of Symbols

A New History of the Picts
Stuart McHardy
ISBN: 978-1-906817-70-1 PBK £8.99

The Picts hold a special place in the Scottish mindset – a mysterious race of painted warriors, leaving behind imposing standing stones and not much more. Stuart McHardy challenges these long-held historical assumptions. He aims to get to the truth of who the Picts really were, and what their influence has been on Scotland's past and present.

McHardy demonstrates that rather than being some historical group of outsiders, or mysterious invaders, the Picts were in fact the indigenous people of Scotland and the most significant of our tribal ancestors. The Picts were not wiped out in battle, but gradually integrated with the Scots to form Alba. Their descendants walk our streets today.

Written and arranged in a way that is both accessible and scholarly, this is an excellent addition to the growing body of work on the Picts.
THE COURIER

On the Trail of Scotland's Myths and Legends
Stuart McHardy
ISBN 978-1-84282-049-0 PBK £7.99

A journey through Scotland's past from the earliest times through the medium of the awe-inspiring stories that were at the heart our ancestors' traditions and beliefs.

As the art of storytelling bursts into new flower, many tales are being told again as they once were. As *On the Trail of Scotland's Myths and Legends* unfolds, mythical animals, supernatural beings, heroes, giants and goddesses come alive and walk Scotland's rich landscape as they did in the time of the Scots, Gaelic and Norse speakers of the past.

This remains an entertaining record of the extent to which history is memorialised in the landscape.
THE SCOTSMAN

Tales of the Picts
Stuart McHardy
ISBN 978-1-842820-97-1 PBK £5.99

For many centuries, the people of Scotland have told stories of their ancestors, a mysterious tribe called the Picts. This ancient Celtic-speaking people, who fought off the might of the Roman Empire, are perhaps best known for their Symbol Stones – images carved into standing stones left scattered across Scotland, many of which have their own stories.

Here, for the first time, these tales are gathered together with folk memories of bloody battles, chronicles of warriors and priestesses, saints and supernatural beings. From Shetland to the Border with England, these ancient memories of Scotland's original inhabitants have flourished since the nation's earliest days and now are told afresh, shedding new light on our ancient past.

Details of these and other books published by Luath Press can be found at:
www.luath.co.uk

Luath Press Limited

committed to publishing well written books worth reading

LUATH PRESS takes its name from Robert Burns, whose little collie Luath (*Gael.*, swift or nimble) tripped up Jean Armour at a wedding and gave him the chance to speak to the woman who was to be his wife and the abiding love of his life. Burns called one of 'The Twa Dogs' Luath after Cuchullin's hunting dog in Ossian's *Fingal*. Luath Press was established in 1981 in the heart of Burns country, and now resides a few steps up the road from Burns' first lodgings on Edinburgh's Royal Mile.

Luath offers you distinctive writing with a hint of unexpected pleasures.

Most bookshops in the UK, the US, Canada, Australia, New Zealand and parts of Europe either carry our books in stock or can order them for you. To order direct from us, please send a £sterling cheque, postal order, international money order or your credit card details (number, address of cardholder and expiry date) to us at the address below. Please add post and packing as follows: UK – £1.00 per delivery address; overseas surface mail – £2.50 per delivery address; overseas airmail – £3.50 for the first book to each delivery address, plus £1.00 for each additional book by airmail to the same address. If your order is a gift, we will happily enclose your card or message at no extra charge.

Luath Press Limited
543/2 Castlehill
The Royal Mile
Edinburgh EH1 2ND
Scotland

Telephone: 0131 225 4326 (24 hours)
email: sales@luath.co.uk
Website: www.luath.co.uk